MUSICAL BRIDGES
Intergenerational Music Programs

JOAN SHAW
CARNA MANTHEY

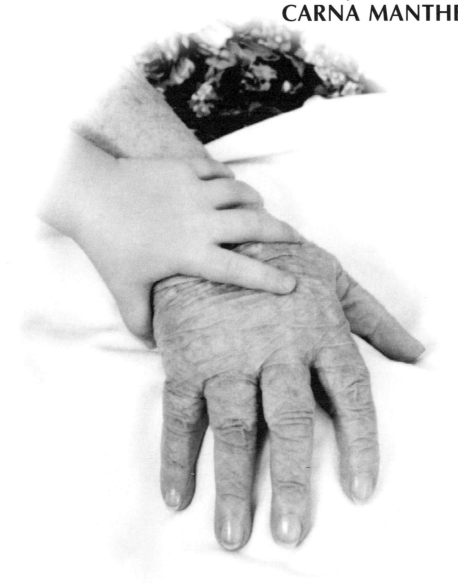

MMB
MMB MUSIC, INC.

> *Every effort has been made to properly credit composers, lyricists, and publishers for songs used throughout this text and to obtain the appropriate reprint permissions where applicable. If any credits or permissions have been inadvertantly overlooked, please contact the publisher at the address below.*

MUSICAL BRIDGES
Intergenerational Music Programs

Joan Shaw, RMT-BC and Carna Manthey, RMT-BC

© Copyright 1996, MMB Music, Inc. All right reserved. International protection secured under Berne, UCC, Buenos Aires, and bilateral copyright treaties. No part of this publication many be reproduced, stored in a retreival system, or transmitted—in any form or by any means now known or later developed—without prior written permission except in the case of brief quotations embodied in critical articles and reviews.

Editor: Carl Simpson
Typesetter: Lynne Condellone
Cover design: Lynne Condellone
Graphics: Roger Shaw
Photography: Ty Manthey
Music examples: Ephraim Jones
Printer: John S. Swift Co., Inc.
First printing: November, 1996
ISBN: 0-918812-90-9
Printed in U.S.A.

For further information and catalogs, contact:

MMB Music, Inc.
Contemporary Arts Building
3526 Washington Avenue
Saint Louis, MO 63101-1019 USA

Phone: 314 531-9635, 800 543-3772 (USA/Canada)
Fax: 314 531-8384
e-mail: mmbmusic@mmbmusic.com
website: http://www.mmbmusic.com

DEDICATION

*Dedicated to everyone
who feels the significance of bridging and overcoming
the generation gap.*

ACKNOWLEDGMENTS

Roger Shaw, the primary illustrator for *Musical Bridges,* is a retired physicist for MEMC Electronic Materials Co. where he did research on the properties of silicon. Upon retirement he joined Joan's interests in geriatrics and began a second career in graphic art on his computer. Joan and Roger enjoyed raising musical children and then were the caretakers for five of their elders. As the "nest" emptied, they moved to the Rocky Mountains where they continue to write and produce graphic art for gerontology books in addition to skiing and backpacking. Evenings, they both perform in several musical organizations, especially at retirement centers.

Ty Manthey, photographer, is a professional lithographer with the Defense Mapping Agency of the United States. His degree is in vocational education graphic communicatons. He taught photography and graphic arts to high school students while in Wisconsin. Ty shares his wife's enthusiasm for her work. He uses his spare time to photograph the intergenerational activities with the results featured in this book.

Heartfelt thanks to the residents of Laclede Commons Assisted Living Center at Laclede Groves and the staff there that contributed so willingly to this book. The cooperation of Janet Fiedler, activities director, and Sharon Rullkoetter, administrator, was truly a pleasure. Everyone enjoyed the interactions with the Webster Groves Child Care Center and we are especially thankful to the staff for their leadership. We are also thankful for the musical, social, and educational contributions of Verdi Morley, Linda Castillon, Myrle Frederick, all music therapists, as well as those of Janilla Ghafoori, a most enthusiastic student.

Special thanks to Delmar Gardens Enterprises, Inc., the executive staff, administrators and activity directors for their continued support of music therapy throughout the years. Without their cooperation this book would not be possible. Gratitude to the following directly involved in intergenerational music programming: residents and staff of Delmar Gardens on the Green Nursing and Rehabilitative Center; children and staff of Kindercare Learning Center of Ballwin, Missouri; residents, staff, and day care children at Delmar Gardens South Nursing and Rehabilitationive Center, to Kathy Vogt, Director of Day Care, and Marge Allen who coordinated programming, shared their ideas and support—making the experience a joy.

TABLE OF CONTENTS

INTRODUCTION vii
HISTORY viii
GENERAL GOAL x

PART ONE: GOALS, NEEDS, PREPARATION

CHAPTER ONE: *GOALS, BENEFITS, NEEDS*
    Benefits of Intergenerational Programs 3
    Needs of Preschool Children 5
    Behavioral Characteristics and Musical Development Chart 6
    Needs of the Elderly 8
    Aspects of Aging and Music Therapy Applications Chart 9
    Music Therapy Goals Between Generations 11
    Successful Music Therapy Ideas 11
    References 13

CHAPTER TWO: *PRACTICAL PREPARATION*
    Initial Encounter 15
    First Session 15
    Practical Planning Ideas 16
    Prolonging the Effects 17
    Equipment Necessary 18
    Room Arrangements 18
    References 20

PART TWO: PROGRAMS

GENERAL FORMAT 25
25 Complete Programs 26-138
Theme and Title
    Program 1. ANIMALS—Animal Fun 26
    Program 2. APPLES—Apples Are A-Peeling 30
    Program 3. BASEBALL—Baseball for All 35
    Program 4. BIRDS—It's For the Birds! 39
    Program 5. BIRTHDAYS—Happy Birthday! 43
    Program 6. CHINESE NEW YEAR—Happy Chinese New Year! 47
    Program 7. CIRCUS—Step Right Up! 51
    Program 8. DOLLS—Dolls Are Different 55
    Program 9. FALL—Autumn Calling 60
    Program 10. FAMILIES—Baby, It's You 66
    Program 11. FLAGS—Our Flag Forever 69
    Program 12. FLYING—Flying High 74

Program 13. HALLOWEEN—Boo to You 78
Program 14. HANDS—Hands Are Handy 82
Program 15. JOBS—Helpful Jobs 86
Program 16. LOVE—I Love You 90
Program 17. SCHOOL—School Bells 96
Program 18. SMILES—Smiles are Super 100
Program 19. OUTER SPACE—Outer Space Is the Place 104
Program 20. SPRING—Spring Fling 108
Program 21. SUMMER—You Are My Sunshine 112
Program 22. THANKSGIVING—Thankful Living 118
Program 23. WEST—Westward Ho 124
Program 24. WHEELS—Wheels Take Us Places 130
Program 25. WINTER—Let It Snow 134

PART THREE: APPENDICES

A. Additional Activities 140
B. Hello and Good-bye Songs 142
C. Useful Form Letters 145
D. Multi-Use Patterns 147
E. Photo Album 150

PART FOUR: RESOURCES

Music Books 152
Intergenerational Books 152
Quotation Sources 154

PART FIVE: INDEX

Song Title Index 157
General Index 159

INTRODUCTION

The creation of *Musical Bridges* developed from the authors' experiences of successfully combining preschool children and retirement and nursing home residents through music and music-based activities. While many intergenerational programs exist and have been described in research and literature, very little exists using MUSIC to span the generations. With day care centers and nursing homes often built adjacent to each other, or housed together, the opportunity to combine these populations is readily available. Now we want you to have this pleasure and privilege.

Music processes melody, rhythms and harmonies on both sides of the brain which accounts for its longevity in the memory bank. *Musical Bridges* frequently uses familiar songs and rhythms since they are easily recalled. This adds to the enjoyment. By adapting just the words, it is easier for everyone to be a part of these musical programs. All effort has been made to give proper credit to composers and lyricists of the listed works. Music and texts for most of the songs cited can be found in the commercially available publications listed in Part Four.

It is the intent of this book to present music-based programs centered on a theme. The basic format is kept throughout so participants and leaders can be comfortable with the structure of each session. Traditional music which spans these generations has been used as well as popular children's songs. "Golden Oldies" are used so that "grandfriends" (as elders are referred to in this book) may pass on their musical heritage. Use your own creativity to include favorite and currently popular music familiar to your own residents and children.

Both the music and the activities are presented for grandfriends and three and four year olds with special adaptations for two year olds to be combined with grandfriends. The material is organized so that anyone working with these populations may implement the programs: activity directors, music therapists, day care teachers, music specialists and recreational directors. Every program allows for positive interactions adding significant memories for all generations. Beginning chapters list the benefits, needs and music goals for each population with suggestions for starting an intergenerational music-based program. It is our hope that your experiences with these programs will bring everyone much joy as you create *Musical Bridges* between the generations.

Joan Shaw and Carna Manthey
Autumn, 1996

HISTORY

Dear Reader,

Little did I realize the impact Joan Shaw would have on my life at our first meeting. Having recently moved to St. Louis in 1981 after 15 years of teaching public school music in Wisconsin, I was looking for a new challenge and career. Aware of the field of music therapy from my college days, I decided to attend the regional Music Therapy conference in St. Louis. Eager to question those attending, I approached the first friendly face I saw. She introduced herself as Joan Shaw, and yes, music therapy was a viable field with job opportunities, she stated. Joan suggested looking into the Maryville College program where she was an instructor. She has been my mentor and dear friend since that first encounter.

With an interest in geriatrics, and degree in hand, I was fortunate to begin private contracting with nursing homes and retirement centers owned by Delmar Gardens Enterprises. One nursing home, Delmar Gardens South, included an in-house day care licensed for 13 preschool children. This afforded me the opportunity to combine my past experience with children with the geriatric population. Intergenerational Music Therapy was born and has developed in many directions in my work. One program developed by Diane Quitmeyer, practicum student from Maryville College, combined 90 year old Lillian Margenau as keyboard accompanist for the children and a small group of residents (see photo.) Another program, still in use, involves selected residents of the Alzheimer's division. A third includes day care children in the last 15 minutes of a large group music therapy session. Realizing the tremendous benefits and success of intergenerational music therapy, a program was developed at another nursing center, Delmar Gardens on the Green, bringing children from an outside day care into the nursing home.

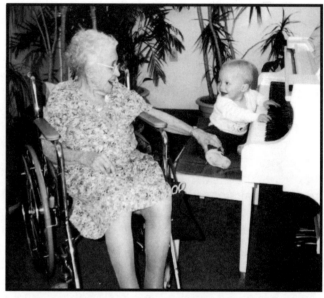
Lillian Margenau and great-grandson, Luke.

Encouraged by Joan Shaw, I began researching intergenerational programs and presented a session on my work in 1993 at the regional NAMT conference in Lawrence, Kansas. Inspired by the results of our work, we decided to combine our efforts to share our experiences through this book. My heartfelt thanks must go to my parents who always supported my love of music and instilled in me an appreciation for intergenerational living by supporting myself, seven brothers and sisters and grandmother under on roof! I wish also to thank my family for their patience and support in this worthwhile effort, and the music shared through the years with our children, Scott and Michelle.

Enthusiastically,

Carna Manthey

Dear Reader,

Watching Carna Manthey in action is quite an experience. Everyone benefits: the preschoolers, the elderly, the staff, the visitors and me, the university music therapy practicum coordinator. I knew her work had to be available for more people in an interesting book format since the world couldn't witness what I had seen and heard that day. My interest was more than a singular experience. My personal life soon became very involved in eldercare with my dear mother Ida, age 87.

Mother lived alone by choice and enjoyed her home and garden until life became too isolated and difficult. After shopping together for the right solution for her situation, she chose an assisted living facility, Laclede Commons in Webster Groves, Missouri. When we walked in the front door there were preschool children in the living room. Some were sitting in the laps of their grandfriends and enjoying books together. Others were just wiggling or resting near the silent grand piano. My mother thoroughly enjoyed seeing the kids and asked me to play something on the piano. The reaction was warm and wonderful. Music did the work of being the catalyst that instantly combined both generations. My future work in music therapy was apparent.

Though numerous experts are in agreement on the great value of intergenerational activities, extensive research failed to turn up any books involving musical activities. After discussions with the administration and activities director, sessions were scheduled immediately. The merriment cannot adequately be described in words. The staff joined in as well as families, music therapy students, visitors and administrators. Ida thrived in such an environment and eagerly shared her vocal talents. Two days before she passed on, she was still able to sing "God Bless America" in spite of severe dementia. You might say she ended on a high note. She blessed us all with her encouragement of this collection of good times.

I wish to express my eternal gratitude to my parents for their years of dedication to my musical escapades and all those concerts they smiled through. Our children, Martha, Gordon, and Bev, receive rave reviews for helping with the editing and singing of these old songs as well as the familiar kids melodies. Lastly, I wish to acknowledge the work of the MMB Music staff and the creativity of the Manthey-Shaw quartet.

It is my hope that this letter regarding the background of these programs will convince you that all it takes is children, grandfriends, music and your enthusiasm. Here is your "how to" book of suggestions along with my best wishes for your success.

Enthusiastically,

Jean Shaw

MUSICAL BRIDGES

General Goal

To create joyous and easily applied bridges between preschoolers and the elderly using music and music-related activites.

PART ONE
GOALS, NEEDS, PREPARATION

"A SOCIETY THAT CUTS OFF OLDER PEOPLE FROM MEANINGFUL CONTACT WITH CHILDREN...... IS GREATLY ENDANGERED. IN THE PRESENCE OF GRANDPARENT AND GRANDCHILD, PAST AND FUTURE MERGE IN THE PRESENT."
— *Margaret Mead*

CHAPTER ONE
Goals, Benefits, Needs

BENEFITS OF INTERGENERATIONAL PROGRAMS

Benefits for both generations
- Increased self-esteem
- The promotion of mutual respect
- The formation of new friendships
- Increased love, touching, and affection
- Increased socialization for the elderly
- Increased social development of the children
- Shared special interests
- Impact of positive intergenerational attitudes
- Opportunity for creativity and self expression
- Interaction of group dynamics
- Cooperation which increases the prestige of any age
- New vocabulary
- Therapy of singing and movement

Benefits for the young
- Greater capacity for patience and responsibility
- Increased listening skills
- Awareness of history as their link to the past
- Positive attitudes toward the elderly
- Supportive environment which aids attitude toward aging and death
- Opportunity to meet elders who have been successful in living
- New resources for academic learning
- New family activities including the songs children bring home
- Chance for small performances for a very receptive older audience
- Opportunity for conversations that are received unconditionally
- Development of motor, social, cognitive, emotional and sensory skills
- Increased and broadened child support system
- Opportunity to observe and become comfortable with various disabilities
- Calming influence of elders to an upset child
- Enhanced respect for individual differences
- Formation of new friendships
- Grandparents or grandfriends

Benefits for the Elderly
- Contribution to the lives of the children
- Lessened depression due to a sense of self worth
- Increased role of involvement in society
- Opportunity to pass life experiences along to the third generation
- Contribution of their time to listening carefully to the children
- Additional learning situations

- Appreciation of their own experiences and knowledge in contrast to the child's
- Awareness of the continuity of life
- Exposure to current trends of children's toys, clothes, foods, attitudes, songs, and interactions
- Observation of current child psychology
- Increased awareness of current child development
- Realization of the changing role of the working parents and changing life styles of the family
- Observation of children interacting with each other
- Improved personal appearances as the children's visit is anticipated
- Restoration of memories of their childhood
- Maintained or increased motor, social, cognitive, emotional and sensory skills
- Anticipation of weekly programs that make life more satisfying
- Opportunity for reminiscences to be shared with a new audience
- Overall quality of life enhanced
- Formation of new friendships
- Chance to enjoy children if they did not have their own
- Joy of childhood without the work

Benefits for the families of both generations

- Decreased generation gap
- Formation of new friendships
- Realization that their child or older adult attends a facility that fosters intergenerational activities
- Increased conversational topics when visiting the elderly or at home
- Positive image to the community that is praiseworthy
- Dispelled stereotypes about aging or present day children
- Awareness that this may be the only program that their older adult participates in regularly
- Shared information and feelings about the children of today and/or growing older
- Opportunity to witness their loved ones in an enjoyable activity
- Privilege of volunteering their expertise or services

Benefits for the staff

- Obvious bridging of the generations
- Opportunity to contribute and participate in well planned activities
- Anticipation of each session
- Cost effective programming
- Increased conversations all week long
- Improved staff morale
- All programs can be charted regarding goals and objectives for state or facility reports regarding participation

Goal, Benefits, Needs

NEEDS OF PRESCHOOL CHILDREN

- To be loved and nurtured
- To be respected
- To be comforted
- To develop a positive and accurate self-concept
- To develop a sense of trust
- To receive praise and positive reinforcement
- To explore all senses
- To interact with objects and other people
- To feel safe and secure
- To have time to develop and grow in a supportive environment
- To have a stimulating learning environment
- To express feelings
- To be physically active in a safe environment
- To play: to engage in parallel play around others until ready for group play
- To experience fine and gross motor activities
- To make safe choices
- To learn to share, cooperate and help when developmentally ready
- To witness positive role models of both sexes
- To have patient listeners

Preschool participation aspects

The preschool years are a period of tremendous development of sensory and motor faculties. They are also very fertile ground for development of attitudes and emotional personality structures which will last a lifetime. Positive experience with any aspect of our social structure at this stage of life will color the entire life view. Attitudes toward the elderly and the aging process are certainly among those that can benefit from this exposure. The programs of this book are intended to give the preschoolers an experience in which the elderly are encountered as friendly, active participants in activities in which they teach the youngsters, share with them and appreciate them. Such young people will be more comfortable in dealing with aging and the aged throughout their lives and more willing and able to help the elderly in need. This is our hope for the young people who are exposed to these intergenerational programs.

Much excellent work has been done on the development of the social and musical capabilities of preschool-age children (see References.) The left hand side of the following chart summarizes the basic behavioral characteristics of children from ages two to four in the areas of social, motor, cognitive, emotional and sensory development. Suggestions for musical applications of these behavioral characteristics to the programs of this book are presented in the right hand column of the chart. Since children mature at varying rates, these are general guidelines to aid in program development.

BEHAVIORAL CHARACTERISTICS & MUSICAL DEVELOPMENT CHART

TWO YEAR OLDS	
BEHAVIORAL CHARACTERISTIC	**MUSIC THERAPY APPLICATION**
Social Development Egocentric: sense of self begins to develop; engages in parallel play Language: words and phrases. Can do one thing at a time—talk vs. action Recognizes familiar songs Songs imitated in order of words, rhythm, and pitch Vocal range develops from A (220) to A (440) Accepts shared attention	Provide materials for all participants; give choice to interact Match actions with words (hello, goodbye) Make up "sing-song" phrases to match play (use minor 3rd interval) Use single word phrases in songs (Old MacDonald - E-I-E-I-O) Imitate animal sounds, stories Use pronouns: I, me, you, mine. Use telephone play, interactive games
Motor Development Mobile including walking and running Often unstable Eye-hand coordination developing High energy, fast paced	Use gross motor activites—movement to music but don't attempt to synchronize to beat Walk, turn, bounce; repeated movements, not sequenctial movements Have grandfriends model movements; Use finger plays, reaching and grasping movements Experiment with rhythm instruments; Use props: balls, bubbles, flags; March, dance, use simple exercises.
Cognitive Development Preoperational stage—object permanence: search for objects that are moved and hidden from view Can imitate past events, remember	Use music games in play—hide rhythm instruments and other props to find Use imitation songs—If You're Happy... clap, stamp, etc.
Emotional Development Mixed dependence and independence Stranger anxiety Developing positive and negative feelings about self Fantasies increase	Use individual names in songs Offer choices in music and activities Use songs with emotions, reinforce self-image Use stories, flannel board activities
Sensory Development Sight: watches and observes people, actions, and objects Auditory: Localizes sounds in environment; will listen to music quietly for several minutes; gross discrimination of pitch (high/low), tempo (fast/slow), intensity (loud/soft).	Use stimulating visual environment—lots of space, bright colors, props, costumes. Use sensory stimulation activities. Provide a variety of music listeing and action experiences. Also provide tactile stimulation with familiar objects (eg. comb, fur, wood)

Goal, Benefits, Needs

THREE AND FOUR YEAR OLDS	
BEHAVIORAL CHARACTERISTIC	**MUSIC THERAPY APPLICATION**

Social Development
  Begins to sense "mine," "yours"
  Self-control increasing
  Understands delayed gratification
  Language: forms sentences; likes to label objects
  Music: sings spontaneous songs; uses melodic contour and rhythm; some intervals correct
	Encourage taking turns, sharing, cooperation
	
	Use songs that label body parts, actions, etc
	
	Use nursery rhymes, finger plays, social music games (e.g. "Ring Around the Rosy")

Motor Development
  More steady and flexible
 	
  Eye-hand coordination more accurate
 	
  Able to move and sing simultaneously
	Encourage movement to rhymes, play songs, parachute play, balls, balloons, etc.
	Use gross and fine motor activities. Rhythm equipment will catch interest.
	Exercise to music

Cognitive Development
  Seek information through manipulation and observation; begin problem solving
  Some understanding of number, space, quantity, time
  Some development of concept understanding
  Highly curious.
	Parachute play directing — "up-down," "in-out," etc.
	Use songs reinforcing concepts (e.g. "Ten Little Indians")

Emotional Development
  Feels positive and negative self-worth
 	
  Strong emotional feelings acted out
	Express appropriate feelings through songs and musical play
	Use positive affirmation. Direct energy through movement

Sensory Development Improved discrimination of pitch, tempo, and intensity	Use sensory stimulation activities

NEEDS OF THE ELDERLY

- To be loved
- To feel a sense of worth
- To contribute
- To share their values
- To have emotional outlets
- To retain their dignity
- To compensate for sensory losses
- To socialize and reduce isolation
- To reaffirm their unique identity
- To understand and cope with depression
- To understand and cope with some memory loss
- To maintain physical well-being
- To feel confident about financial concerns
- To fulfill spiritual needs
- To have learning opportunities
- To live in a comfortable environment
- To experience security
- To participate in meaningful activities
- To have adequate nutrition
- To interact with other generations
- To experience the art of growing older gracefully

Geriatric participation aspects

Whether you refer to the older population as seniors, senior citizens, the elderly, oldsters, maturians, or seasoned citizens, they deserve respect and dignity. "An old person is simply one who has lived a long time" says Hugh Downs. Sometimes this involves disabilities or social adjustment problems.

The chart on the following pages presents some common bio-physical aspects of aging that are encountered in day care, retirement, senior citizen or nursing home facilities. Each aspect is described briefly with a music therapy application or two on the right side of the chart. The musical applications are based on research as well as experience by both authors. Many more musical activities are appropriate. This book lists only a few ideas for each medical concern.

We ask that readers not get depressed with all of the medical and social concerns of aging but realize that music can alleviate and sometimes even heal these conditions. S.C. Lewis has proven that by effectively structuring the social and physical environment, the individual can continue to live a productive and satisfying life. These twenty-five programs will enliven any facility with satisfying experiences.

Social adjustment is possible by reflecting on the past and enjoying the present. Older people have survived childhood diseases, accidents, emotional problems, financial insecurity, raising families and other challenges. Now they can share their experiences as well as the energy of the youngsters. This book is intended to present flexible programs that will be of interest to older people since it involves the interaction with children using music as the modality to bridge the generations.

Our older grandfriends can offer much to the children due to their years of wisdom and experience, but someone has to provide the opportunity for intergenerational interaction. We hope it is you.

ASPECTS OF AGING & MUSIC THERAPY APPLICATIONS CHART

BIO-PHYSICAL ASPECTS	MUSIC THERAPY APPLICATION
Central Nervous System Loss of brain tissue and short term memory Decreased motor coordination Shorter endurance time Uneven gait Ability to learn new information difficult Decrease in reflex response time	Use familiar songs, simple response songs, short versions of music Use omnichord, autoharp, rhythm instruments Plan interesting programs involving audience Work with physical therapist for appropriate gait, exercise to music at that tempo Teach new, short songs and praise everyone Slow yourself down, allow more time for their responses to musical activities
Sensory Aspects Impaired vision Ability to smell and taste lessens Gradual hearing loss Decreased nerve fibers in the ear causing unsteady balance and falls	Use large print songsheets or memorize one verse Admit losses, accentuate the senses that do work. Reminisce with songs about smells and taste. Laugh a lot Use a microphone. Speak clearly and directly Participants seated with all musical programs planned within their movement capabilities
Musculoskeletal System Spinal column less flexible, poorer posture Muscle strength declines	Encourage sitting straighter when singing for better physical and singing results Use chime bars, bell choirs, rhythm bands
Cardiovascular System Changes in heart rate, increase in blood pressure, blood volume decreases about age eighty	Offer music with a steady, even beat to provide order in internal bodily rhythms
Pulmonary System Less efficient respiratory system, reduced elasticity of the lungs, decrease in activity	Encourage deep breathing before singing. Use songs in appropriate keys—A below middle C to A above middle C recommended
Digestive System Fewer calories required, good diet essential	Use relaxed, familiar dinner music to aid digestion and increase conversation
Genitourinary System Elasticity of bladder decreases causing more trips to the bathroom	Plan on bathroom facilities nearby for all age groups

PSYCHOLOGICAL ASPECTS	MUSIC THERAPY APPLICATION
Depression 　Low self-esteem 　Irritability 　Social withdrawal 　Sleep disturbance 　Inablility to concentrate	Use individual names in songs Schedule individual session, match mood with music and slowly uplift with livelier tempo Invite personally to the group session for five minutes or to sit in the back and observe Provide soothing, relaxing tapes Use familiar music with rhythmic responses
Anxiety Disorders 　Feelings of confusion, helplessness	Match their mood with a meaningful song then rewrite the song together with positive values Reminisce with familiar music while praising their longevity.

ORGANIC DISORDERS	MUSIC THERAPY APPLICATION
Senile Dementia 　Progressive memory loss 　Loss of emotional response 　Mini strokes possible 　Personal appearance unimportant 　Reduced attention span 　Wandering and pacing	React slowly, calmly. Familiar music once initiated is often very successful Use of live music, babies, animals Use music activities with calm movements Use program props and costumes; Use mirrors Use simple music, shorter sections, props to increase sensory stimulation Not appropriate to involve them in a group session. Individual attention best
Alzheimer's Disease 　Decline in cognitive functions, lapses in judgment, decline in personal hygiene, bizarre thought patterns, overall general deterioration	Use rhythmic and movement activities; Use lots of props such as scarves, balloons, tactile stimulants, positive affirmations, accent their names in songs; Use music of younger years to aid recall; Involve families since music can be the only way to reach some stages

MUSIC THERAPY GOALS BETWEEN GENERATIONS

Music therapy is the planned use of music to reach nonmusical goals. These programs establish intergenerational relationships through the use of music. The list below provides specific goals that can be attained and documented. If even a few of these goals are reached with any one program, satisfaction is derived.

- Interaction between both groups
- Communication promoted but not required
- Increased self esteem
- Awareness of present age and stage
- Participation at one's own level
- Creative expression
- Decision making opportunities
- Development and/or maintenance of physical coordination
- Stimulation of cognitive thinking and development
- Exposure of children to nurturing adults
- Stimulation of memory recall using familiar, old melodies
- Learning about self in this environment
- Meet social and emotional needs through concepts of sharing
- Increased memory and attention span
- Stimulation of visual and auditory senses
- Increased childs understanding of aging
- Familiarization of the elderly with today's children
- Reinforcement of positive learning experiences
- Elders culture shared and passed on to the younger generation
- Enjoyment of a live, positive session using music as the catalyst
- Introduction and promotion of family activities using music
- Extension of exercise period with rhythmic activities
- Encouragement of automatic physiological responses with rhythmic activities
- Maintenance and development of music skills
- Introduction and encouragement of new musical instruments

SUCCESSFUL MUSIC THERAPY IDEAS

- Use children's songs including nursery rhymes that are familiar to all—they restore cherished memories and are easily recognized by the children
- Use chants for group unity and children's leadership in presenting the alphabet
- Use finger plays for finger exercise, first as a chant, then add the music
- Let the children teach their grandfriends one of their songs to keep them current with new music
- Expose children to some "Golden Oldies" with positive lyrics
- Print songs in large print for all to take home and share with others
- Include music and/or words or take home sheets only if not copyrighted
- Teach by rote rather than the awkwardness of song sheets
- Use familiar or adapted songs
- One verse sung twice is easily remembered. Use repetition
- The leader sings the various refrains and verses while the group learns only the chorus
- Plan on an appropriate singing key that is comfortable for all
- The vocal range for both groups is approximately A to A above middle C
- Allow choices

- Use large motions, one at a time for action songs
- Use props to aid spontaneity with the combination of music
- As the children enter the session, have live or recorded music playing
- Slow tempos are preferred especially when learning a song
- Always open with a Hello song using individual names if possible—see examples.
- Plan on children marching around the elders chairs with their teacher leading.
- Use live music with its vibrant energy whenever you have a choice.
- Plan on someone leading the music if you are the accompanist.
- If working from the piano, use a microphone.
- Children dancing is a welcome sight; grandfriends can do it vicariously.
- Request good equipment including a tuned piano and safe rhythm instruments.
- Use songs that include the words, "you," "me," and "us" to link generations musically and socially
- Programs with a theme should have related music
- Conclude with a good-bye song and announce the date and time of the next session (see examples)
- Encourage everyone to keep on singing and humming every day
- Use familiar, simple songs
- Simple or no accompaniment is best

We've got rhythm!

Let's make music, yes indeed!

REFERENCES

Andress, B.: *Music Experiences in Early Childhood.* New York, NY, 1980: Holt, Rinehart, Winston.
   Describes the developmental growth of the child and how music can become an integral part of the growth sequence. Stresses the role of the teacher in musical development and claims that the child does not learn music through just one approach. The book includes a variety of sound sources and easily made instruments.

Barrickman, Joey, RMT-BC: "A Developmental Music Therapy Approach for Preschool Hospitalized Children" in *Music Therapy Perspectives,* Vol. 7. 1989: (pp. 10-13)
   Normal musical and non-musical development of 2, 3, and 4 year old children. Outlines development in motor activity, movement, musical sound discrimination and social development.

Bayless, K.M. and Ramsey, M.E.: *Music: A Way of Life for the Young Child.* St. Louis, MO, 1982: C.V. Mosby Co.
   Selected physical and social characteristics of two, three and four year olds with related activities. Book also includes printed music popular with this age group.

Bright, Ruth. *Music Therapy and the Dementias.* St. Louis, MO, 1988: MMB Music, Inc. Introduction, (pp iv-vi) "How Music Therapy Helps Dementing Persons." (pp 22-42), "Music for Recreation and Fun." (pp. 55-57)
   Excellent book describing the effect of the dementias on the client, observers and care givers with suggestions for creative activities infused with hope.

Brummel, Steven W.: "Developing an Intergenerational Program" in *Journal of Children in Contemporary Society,* Vol. 20, Nos. 3-4, 1989: (pp. 119-133)
   Rationale for developing programs including this book.

Butler, Robert, MD and Lewis, M.: *Aging and Mental Health: Positive Psychosocial Approaches.* St. Louis, MO, 1973: C.V. Mosby Co.
   Excellent chapters: 2. Healthy Successful Old Age, 3. Common Emotional Problems, 4. Functional Disorders, 5. Organic Brain Disorders and 8 General Treatment Principles. Quote on "elder function" p. 24.

Coni, Nicolas, Davison, William, and S. Webster: *Aging: the Facts*, New York, 1984. Oxford University Press. Chapter 6. Normal Aging. (pp. 44-54) Chapter 7. Psychology of Aging. (pp.55-60)
   Describes the mobility and immobility of sensory changes and diseases.

Crites, Martha S.: "Child Development and Intergenerational Programming" in *Journal of Children in Contemporary Society.* New York, NY, 1989: Haworth Press. (pp. 33-38)
   Connection between human development and intergenerational relationships including programming. Focus on the four developmental stages and ways older adults can foster them.

Daum, M. and Gretzel, G.: *Preference for Age-Homogeneous versus Age-Heterogeneous Social Interaction,* paper presented at the 1980 Annual Scientific Meeting of the Gerontological Society.
   People over age sixty-five expressed a preference for interaction with people other than their own age.

Davis, William, Gfeller, Kate, and Thaut, Michael: *Music Therapy: Theory and Practice,* Dubuque, IA, 1992: William C. Brown.
   "Populations Served by Music Therapists, Music Therapy and Elderly Populations." (pp. 133-196)
Excellent presentation of the general bio-physical, psychosocial issues and age related disorders often experienced by older persons. Basis for the chart of Aspects of Aging and Music Therapy Applications.

Downs, Hugh: *Fifty to Forever.* Nashville, TN,1994: Thomas Nelson, Inc. Quote by Satchel Paige (pp. 13)
   Excellent book on becoming older with pride. Includes the famous 30 dirty lies about aging as well as current demographics and statistics.

Johnson, Sallie, and Ginnane, Patrick: "Intergenerational Education: Variations on a Theme" in *Beginnings,* Spring 1985: (pp. 8-12)
   Value of youngsters becoming familiar with people who have lived a long time.

Lambert, Donna. Dellmann-Jenkins, Mary, and Fruit, Dorothy: "Planning for Contact Between Generations; an Effective Approach" in *Gerontologist,* Vol. 30, No. 4, Aug. 1990 (pp. 553-557)
   Research and summary of the positive impact of an intergenerational program in the behavior of the children toward elderly persons.

Leitner, M.: "The Effects of intergenerational Music Activities on Senior Day Care Participants and Elementary School Children," *Dissertation Abstracts International* Vol. 42, No. 8, 1981. (p. 372A)
   Attitudes of children toward older persons became more positive after intergenerational activities.

Manthey, Carna: *Music Therapy in Intergenerational Planning,* seminar at the Midwest Regional Conference of the National Association of Music Therapy, Lawrence, KS. March, 1993.
   She listed the benefits for intergenerational programming and devised the chart of Behavioral Characteristics of Children and the corresponding music therapy applications.

Mersereau, Yvonne, and Glover, Mary: *A Guide to Community.* Madison, WI, 1992: Bi-Folkal Productions, Inc.
   Intergenerational benefits, goals and philosophy well expressed in this book. The book involves young people and nursing home residents. It is well written and inspires one to initiate a program. Preparation clearly defined as well activities and evaluation.

Miller, Karen: *Treatment with Music.* Kalamazoo, MI, 1979: Department of Occupational Therapy, College of Health and Human Services, Western Michigan University.
   Developmental description and musical activities from birth through age eight. Lists many specific goals with corresponding treatment techniques.

Newman, Sally, Lyons, Charles, and Onawola, Roland: "The Development of an Intergenerational Service-Learning Program at a Nursing Home," in *Gerontologist* 1985. (p. 130)
   Improved social and physical conditions of the elderly and in the students perception of aging.

Powell, J.A., and Arquitt, G.: "Getting the Generations Back Together" in *The Family Coordinator,* Vol. 3, No. 10, 1980. (pp. 421-426)
   Rationale for future generations. Children's attitudes toward the aged are a major influence in how older persons will be treated in the future society.

Seefeldt, C.: "Intergenerational Programs: Making Them Work" in *Childhood Education,* Vol. 4, No. 1, 1987. (pp. 14-18)
   Rationale, value of caring connections, research evidence. This article is inspirational.

Shaw, Joan: *The Joy of Music in Maturity.* St. Louis, MO, MMB Music, Inc. Chapter 1. Joy of Organization. (pp. 8-13) Chapter 2. Purpose and Preparation (pp. 15-23.) Part Two. Program Ideas for 80 themes.
   The wonderful experiences this book provided for me as well as others inspired me to extend the joy of programming to include more children and co-author an intergenerational book.

Shotwell, Rita: *Rhythmic and Movement Activities.* "Philosophy, Objectives, Helpful Hints for Early Childhood Music Experiences." (pp. 3-4)

Weiner, Marcella, Brok, A., and Snadowsky, A.: *Working with the Aged: Approaches in the Institution and Community,* Englewood Cliffs, NJ, 1979: Prentice Hall, Inc.
   Normal personality development in old age, sensory training, remotivation techniques, additional therapeutic approaches.

Williams, Mark E. MD: *American Geriatric Society's Complete Guide to Aging and Health,* New York, NY, 1995: Harmony Books. Part One. "How our Body Ages." (pp. 14-33) "How our Mind Changes with Aging." (pp. 33-44)
   The most current geriatric manual available for the layman to understand. Includes a section on aspects of aging that we can influence.

CHAPTER TWO
Practical Preparation

INITIAL ENCOUNTER

For the Elderly

- Prepare a written proposal on the benefits of intergenerational programs for your first meeting
- Propose an intergenerational scheduled program by meeting with the administrator, Director of Nurses and Activity Director and receive their input and approval
- Leave the written proposal with them for their consideration
- Include a sample 30-minute program as well as a 45-minute program
- When approved, meet with the resident council and present the same handouts
- Discuss potential group to invite for this activity such as a nearby day care center, school, church preschool or an in house center for employees children
- Discuss which family members or volunteers should be included
- Choose an appropriate area large enough for movement activities, use of loudspeaker if necessary and nearby bathroom facilities
- Learn specific information regarding participants dietary restrictions
- Obtain information on participants physical limitations

With the Preschoolers

- Contact the administrator and other staff members that may be interested
- Meet with them personally
- Provide written rationale and program for their consideration.
- Set a date for their decision.
- Suggest they meet where the elderly live (Research proves this is most effective)
- Set weekly or bi-weekly sessions for bonding
- Discuss availability of children during the morning for a 45-minute program
- Administrators should choose the same children regularly or rotate classes with your approval
- Once approved, set the date, time and room
- Arrange for committed staff to assist or use interested family members and volunteers
- Work with administrators to send a letter of introduction to the children's families
- Obtain permission to participate and a release form for photos
- Arrange for transportation
- Have a session at school with preschoolers on what to expect with their new grandfriends, including disabilities, longevity, and new friendships
- Discuss their fears and concerns
- Arrange for a tour of the site chosen and a mini-program of introduction, if possible

FIRST SESSION

- Send invitations to the premier of the Intergenerational Program including place, time, and date
- Publicize in house with a poster and notice in your facility newsletter
- Pre-arrange props through the activity departments of both facilities

- Arrange props before the initial program
- Provide background music as residents arrive to add to the atmosphere of a musical program
- Ask the older residents to arrive early—anticipate the children's arrival with discussion and a relaxing rehearsal provided in each program of this book
- Play music related to the program on the piano or tape recorder as children enter and place their coats in a designated area.
- Have children sit on the floor with their teacher; two-year-olds sit on a large blanket that designates the music area with their teacher.
- Let the shy children linger with their teacher.
- Introduce yourself and welcome everyone to this historic session.
- Open with the same welcome song every time for familiarity; make copies for all to take home
- Allow flexibility in every program
- The closing song should also be consistent to signal closure
- Announce the date, time, place and theme of the next session
- Thank all who assisted and attended
- Charting of attendance, participation and significant changes in behavior is done by the staff of both facilities
- Review the session with the residents after the children leave. Later do the same with the staff and administration to prepare for the next program
- Remember the first session is mainly introductory; programs flow more smoothly with experience and longer friendships

PRACTICAL PLANNING IDEAS

Before the session

- Know both populations: developmental stages and readiness of children, abilities of the elderly
- Focus on the common interests of both groups when structuring activities
- Have the children come to the senior center
- Schedule morning hours as they are more successful for intergenerational activities
- Include sensory stimulation activities—they are good for both populations
- Sessions with a theme are easiest to plan and to make cohesive
- Use props as visual stimulation—it helps with elders' recall/associations and gives a focus for the children
- Use a large blanket for the two-year-olds; the seating arrangement is important—see chart
- Request an extra staff member to be present for emergencies and charting.
- Plan a specific area for coats
- Use volunteers and staff members to ease your leadership; let them know their role
- Train assistants to prompt from behind by guiding more than by talking

For the session

- Establish a trusting relationship by getting involved personally with everyone
- Speak slowly and clearly in a relaxed manner
- Use a microphone for large groups—the children enjoy it after familiarity
- Use body language by using eye contact, smiles, and touch
- Be very adaptable and flexible within the structure

Practical Preparation

- Use repetition in your verbal instruction and music activities
- Use simple accompaniments
- Encourage one to one interaction
- Let the children deliver visual aids, or obtain answers from the grandfriends
- Don't over stimulate; keep distractions to a minimum
- Remove crying babies or agitated elders
- Keep session 20-30 minutes for two-year-olds, 45 minutes for three- and four-year-olds
- Keep directives and reinforcements coming from the leader
- Use directives to describe exactly what you are going to do next to eliminate anxiety
- Use reinforcement techniques: tell what is "good," be specific, use frequently, act natural, and be sure it is age appropriate

After the session

- Arrange a specific meeting time to discuss the previous session
- Evaluate the effects on both generations
- Use techniques such as interviews, weekly logs, recorded responses, photographs, resident surveys, observation, staff and parent feedback for evaluation
- Consider video taping the next session for an unbiased evaluator to view
- Review the space allotted
- Review the length of your program
- Review the day chosen and its practicality for both generations
- Discuss future equipment that may be necessary
- Look at the long range results over time for change in the children's attitude and behavior toward the elderly
- Start planning for the next intergenerational session including publicity

PROLONGING THE EFFECTS

- Enjoy promoting your work—the world needs to hear more good news
- Use promotional material such as posters, flyers and announcements regularly
- Write out songs or just lyrics for taking home and enjoying (Appendix A)
- Encourage families to sing these songs during the week
- Encourage the elderly to sing all week long and share these good songs with their grandchildren
- Urge the staff to sing more often or hum songs used in your programs for recall
- Collect your songs and assemble them in a booklet or special folder for each person
- Suggest that everyone listen to many forms of music during the week and talk about it
- Develop creativity by suggesting they create new lyrics during the week
- Invite administrators and other important staff members as guests
- Invite a local newspaper or television reporter
- Find a resident photographer or volunteer and give them this official job with title
- Collect photographs in an album that can be viewed by the public anytime
- Post pictures, songs, handouts for all the world to see the interaction
- Videotape your sessions; get administrative approval first and the individual OKs
- Invite community speakers, musicians, politicians to implement your theme
- Extend sessions with related theme music played during meal hours
- Tape the songs for the children to take back to their school
- Notify relatives about your program; invite them to come or to assist you
- Encourage the elderly to reminisce on the current theme and talk about it during the week

- Write down some of the reactions and post or publish them in house or locally
- Invite another pre-school or senior group to join in the merriment

EQUIPMENT NECESSARY

- Portable music cart
- Acoustic piano or electronic portable keyboard using batteries or adapter
- Guitar for accompaniment
- Omnichord or autoharp for accompaniment
- Microphone for large groups
- Tape recorder and tape collection
- Name tags for children
- Rhythm instruments: tambourines, castanets, bells, shakers. sticks, triangles
- One pair of small cymbals
- Bass drum head
- Large United States flag
- Plastic bird whistles
- Paper plates
- Construction paper
- Inflatable plastic balls, bat
- Helium balloons
- Large blanket for two-year-olds' music area
- Assistants, volunteers, happy hearts
- See individual programs for related props

ROOM ARRANGEMENTS

1. Determine the approximate number who might be attending:

Children _____ Grandfriends _____ Staff _____ Aides _____ Visitors _____
Approximate grand total _____

- It is best to have a ratio of more elderly people than children
- A ratio of 20 adults to 8 to 10 children works best

2. Both facilities should agree on the location after considering the following:
   - The facility where the elderly meet is preferred to the children's center due to the energy of the children and ease in transporting them
   - A large area to accommodate all those attending
   - Space enough for activities involving movement
   - Adequate lighting and heating is important
   - Room availability on a regular basis lessens confusion
   - Nearby noise is at a minimum
   - Bathrooms are close to the planned area
   - Space for coats, hats, umbrellas and treasures
   - Seating for every adult
   - Seating for children optional

Practical Preparation

- List your site possibilities_____ or _____.

3. Once the site is determined plan on arranging the room as follows:
   - Semicircle seating for the adults is preferred
   - Leave a large space for the children to sit in the center when they enter
   - Use small chairs or an area rug if the facility is not carpeted
   - Place a blanket in the center to mark the area for the two-year-old children
   - Place a microphone with a long cord for interviews near your piano or focal point
   - Equipment and props can be put on a roll-away cart. Plan on locked storage for this

4. Decide on a convenient time for both age groups. Mornings are preferable for higher energy level and alertness

   Day of week_____time_____

   - Consider the logistics of transportation.
   - Consider 45-minute programs for three- and four-year-olds, 30 minutes for two-year-olds
   - Grandfriends should arrive first and take their place in the semicircle; if using two rows have your more active people in the front row
   - Greet each person individually
   - Enjoy a relaxing rehearsal of the music planned for the day
   - Use taped or live background music as the children enter
   - Children should sit in the central area on the floor or rug

5. Don't be surprised if:
   - Some people don't participate, especially the first time
   - The room arrangements may need relocating or altering
   - Your program gets interrupted for various reasons; keep to your theme and enjoy the spontaneity of intergenerational programming
   - Your group becomes very popular and oversized; it is best to break it into two groups that meet at separate times
   - The grandfriends request a trip to visit the children's facility; make the arrangements for a tour or joint program there—however, it is wise to be consistent with your location
   - You need to evaluate your program and change the frequency; weekly or bi-weekly is suggested

SESSION SEATING PLAN

- The children with teachers are seated on the floor (or on blankets for the two-year-olds) in the central area of the room
- Grandfriends are arrayed around them or in rows behind, if necessary.
- If there is more than one row of grandfriends, leave room between them for children to circulate individually and in parades; an aisle or two as shown gives parades even more possibilities.
- Ask volunteers or aids to work behind the grandfriends to prompt and help with props and questions
- Keep the equipment far enough from the chlidren to avoid distracting play during the program

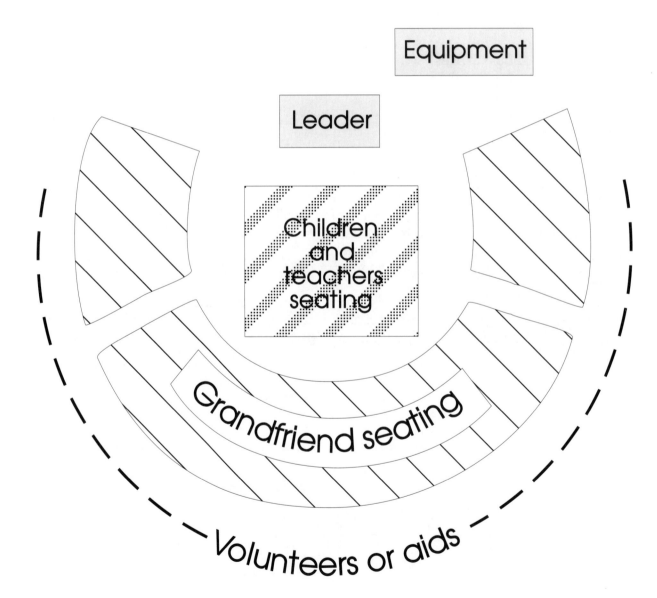

REFERENCES

Amir, Y.: "Contact Hypothesis in Ethnic Relations" in *Psychological Bulletin*, Vol. 71, (pp. 319-342) 1969.
Conditions necessary for interaction between groups

Burnside, Irene: "Themes in Reminiscence Groups" in *International Journal of Aging and Human Development*, Vol. 37 No. 3, 1993. (pp. 177-189)

Chavin, Melanie: *The Lost Chord: Reaching the Person with Dementia Through the Power of Music.*
Mt. Airy, MD, 1992. ElderSong Press. (pp. 7-43)
Brief overview of the dementias, common behavior problems, nonverbal communication techniques, program development and adaptations using music effectively.

Crites, Martha S.: "Child Development and Intergenerational Programming" in *Journal of Children in Contemporary Society,* New York, NY 1989: Haworth Press. (pp. 33-38)
Connection between human development and intergenerational relationships including programming. Focus on the four developmental stages and ways older adults can foster them.

Dezan, Nancy: *Barbers, Cars and Cigars.* Mt. Airy, MD, 1992. ElderSong Press. (pp. 6-8)
Intergenerational programming for men. Helpful suggestions of timing, number attending, first encounter and seven programs.

Karras, Beckie: *Down Memory Lane.* Mt. Airy, MD, 1985, ElderSong Press. ,"Moving Along;" (pp. 67-70) "Working" (pp. 144-147)
Fine book filled with numerous program ideas for the elderly. A classic for programming.

Karras, Beckie: *Moments to Remember: Sequel to Down Memory Lane,* Mt. Airy, MD, 1989: ElderSong Press. "Circus" (pp. 13-15); "Gardening" (pp. 45-48); "Seasons" (pp. 92-103)
Additional programs for older people that are stimulating, musical and enjoyable.

Karras, Beckie: *With a Smile and a Song,* Mt. Airy, MD, 1988: ElderSong Press. (pp. 2-6)
Suggestions for sing-alongs and music for the impaired older adult. Seventy-three pages of themes, songs and the dates the music was popular.

Mason-Luckey, Betsy, and Sandel, Susan: "Intergenerational Movement Therapy; a Leadership Challenge" in *The Arts in Psychotherapy,* Vol. 12, 1985. (pp. 257-262)

Mersereau, Yvonne and Glover and Mary: *A Guide to Community: An Intergenerational Friendship Program.* Madison WI, 1990: Bi-Folkal Productions, Inc., (pp. 5-51)
Getting started, preparing the participants, activities, evaluation

Newman, Sally, Lyons, Charles, and Onawola, Roland: "The Development of an Intergenerational Service-Learning Program at a Nursing Home" in *Gerontologist*, 1985. (pp. 130)
Improved social and physical conditions of the elderly and in the students perception of aging.

Oakwood Hospital Corporation: *The Realities of Intergenerational Planning.* NAMT Conference handout. Oakwood Hospital, Dearborn, MI, 1994.
Lists the benefits of intergenerational planning for the agency, the children and adults.

Robbert, L.: *Bringing Preschoolers and the Institutionalized Elderly Together: How One Program Works.* 1981: Eric Document Reproduction Service. (No. ED 212374)
It is better to take the children to a retirement center complex than to depend on the elderly visiting their school.

Seefeldt, Carol: "The Effects of Preschoolers Visits to a Nursing Home" in *The Gerontologist,* Vol. 67, No. 2, 1987. (pp. 228-232)

Seefeldt, Carol: "Intergenerational Programs-Impact on Attitudes" in *Journal of Children in Contemporary Society*. Vol. 20, No. 3-4. 1989. (pp. 185-194)

Seefeldt, Carol: "Intergenerational Programs: Making Them Work" in *Childhood Education*. Vol. 4, No. 1, 1987. (pp. 14-18)
Rationale, value of caring connections, limited evidence unavailable, research evidence.

Seefeldt, Carol and Warman, Barbara: *Young and Old Together*, Washington, DC, 1990: National Association for the Education of Young Children. (pp. 1-21)
    Fine source book for intergenerational curriculum for children, establishing programs, evaluation, cirriculum materials and resources.

Shaw, Joan: *The Joy of Music in Maturity,* St. Louis, MO, MMB Music, Inc. Chapter 1. Joy of Organization, Expanding Your Staff, Publicizing Your Theme, Cost and Equipment (pp 8-13) Chapter 2. Purpose and Preparation (pp 15-25)
    Previous experiences with children in the nursing center were valuable in setting up the ideal arrangements and format for an intergenerational program.

Shotwell. Rita: "Inter-generational Programs" in *Orff Echo.* November 1985, (pp. 25)
    In 1985 the six suggestions for programming in this paper inspired us to involve the children.

Shotwell, Rita: *Rhythm and Movement Activities for Early Childhood,* West Nyack, NY, 1984: Parker Publishing Co., Inc.
    Fingerplays, use of rhythmic instruments, chants and singing.

Warren, Jean: *Piggyback Songs for Infants and Toddlers,* Everett, WA, 1985. Totline Press.
    New songs sung to the tunes of childhood favorites

Wirth, Marian, Stassevitch, Verna, Shotwell, Rita, and Stemmler, Patricia: *Musical Games, Fingerplays and Rhythmic Activities for Early Childhood,* West Nyack, NY, 1983: Parker Publishing Co., Inc.
    One hundred twenty active music games and fingerplays.

PART TWO
PROGRAMS

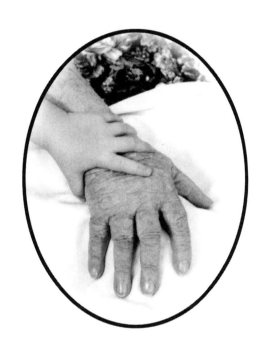

Generations on Parade

PART TWO
General Format

The following twenty-five programs use this basic format for familiarity and structure. It is presented here so you will enjoy creating your own programs.

Program No.: THEME

PREPARATION

MUSIC

GREET SENIORS

RELAXING REHEARSAL

OPENING SONG

MUSICAL WARM UP

INTERACTIVE SONGS AND/OR ACTIVITIES

MARCH/MOVEMENT

COOL DOWN

CLOSING MUSIC

ANNOUNCEMENTS

OPTIONAL ACTIVITY

ADAPTATIONS FOR TWO-YEAR-OLDS

RESOURCES

ANIMAL FUN

Program 1: ANIMALS

PREPARATION: Items include a letter written to children's parents requesting they bring a stuffed animal (no dolls) to the next program, collection of additional animals for props and to pass out to the grandfriends, adult straw hat, rake or pitchfork, apron, mixing bowl, spoon, teddy bear, stuffed cat, mouse and dog, platter of pre-cut cheese for all, collection of rhythm instruments.

MUSIC: "Old MacDonald Had a Farm," "Hey Diddle Diddle," "Pop Goes the Weasel," "Oh Where, O Where Has My Little Dog Gone," "Me and My Teddy Bear," and "Mary Had a Little Lamb."

GREET SENIORS: One on one before children enter.

RELAXING REHEARSAL:
Review the nursery rhyme songs about animals. Ask if they can name any others.

OPENING SONG: Choose your favorite.

MUSICAL WARM UP: Children introduce their animal on the microphone, if possible. If a real microphone is not obtainable, use a fake microphone of a foam ball on a stick. Add a long cord.

- Children or adults pass out stuffed animals to grandfriends from the leaders collection. All are interchangeable, however some may not want to part with theirs.
- Exercise using the stuffed animals in hand so everyone can see them
- Music: "Pop Goes the Weasel"
  Everyone sings while holding their animal and popping it up at the right time. Repeat.

"Oh Where, Oh Where Has My Little Dog Gone?"— Sway animals side to side.
"Hey Diddle, Diddle" (the cat) — Raise animals up and down to the beat.
"Me and My Teddy Bear"— Make circles with the animals.

INTERACTIVE SONGS AND/OR ACTIVITIES: Both generations play "Farmer in the Dell" together. Those participating can place the animals in one area to watch the activity. Children form a circle and go around singing allowing time for each new person to enter the song and the ring. Children choose a farmer and give him a straw hat and pitchfork. Everyone sings the song "The Farmer in the Dell." Follow the words of the song using props.

ANIMAL FUN

The farmer takes a wife. He chooses a woman. (apron, mixing bowl, spoon)
The wife takes a child. She chooses a child. (teddy bear)
The child takes a dog. Someone small gets on all fours and barks. (may carry a stuffed dog)
The dog takes the cat. Someone small gets on all fours and meows. (may carry a toy cat)
The cat takes the rat. Let child choose anyone. (catnip mouse)
The rat takes the cheese. Surprise everyone with a platter of chunks of cheese or a treat.

While everyone is eating, take a group picture of the farmer's family.

Place all animals together in one area to watch the rhythm band. Children can assist in passing out rhythm instruments to their grandfriends and keeping one for themselves. Use the music to "Old MacDonald Had a Farm" only substitute musical instruments for the animals:

Example:
On his farm he had some bells, E-I-E-I-O
With a ring, ring, here and a ring, ring there.....

Sing about the rest of the instruments in your collection ending with "Old MacDonald has a band, E-I-E-I-O, and in his band he has everyone, E-I-E-I-O with music here and music there, music, music, everywhere, Old MacDonald had a band, E-I-E-I-O.

Collect all the instruments and have the children pick up their own animals.

MARCH/MOVEMENT: Children march to the tune of the "Mickey Mouse March".

The Farmer in the Dell

"I'm learning 'new' old songs."

— *Everett, age 86; and Ben, age 3*

ANIMAL FUN

COOL DOWN: Children seated with their animals. Ask everyone to guess the name of the animal in the following songs played on the piano, taped or even sung. Yell out the answer:

"Mary Had a Little Lamb"
"Rudolph the Red Nosed Reindeer"
"Baa, Baa Black Sheep"
"Hickory, Dickory Dock" (mouse)
"Jingle Bells" (horse)
"Three Blind Mice"

CLOSING MUSIC: Use the same song each session.

ANNOUNCEMENTS: Thank everyone for sharing their animals. Suggest they talk about animals and pets they like the best later in the day.

OPTIONAL ACTIVITY: Interactive song—use the name of the teacher instead of MacDonald.

ADAPTATIONS FOR TWO-YEAR-OLDS

Interactive Songs and/or Activities: Replace the Farmer in the Dell activity with the song "Mary Had a Little Lamb." Group singing followed by using the child's name and the animal they are holding. For example, _____ had a little bear, little bear, little bear _____ had a little bear, it was lot's of fun.

Ask the child to share it with a grandfriend using their name in the song. Continue until all the children have a chance to be identified and given the opportunity to share with the grandfriends.

Felt board activity—Use the pictures corresponding to the "Farmer in the Dell" (included)

RESOURCES:

Children's Songbook
   All of the songs

For additional ideas see *The Joy of Music in Maturity*
   "Animal Friends" p. 305-309

THE FARMER IN THE DELL

APPLES are A-PEELING

Program 2: APPLES

PREPARATION: Items needed include pre-cut apple name tags (pattern included) or bookmarks for everyone, hand baskets, apron, rolling pin, bushel basket, apple peeler, and apples (or apple butter on crackers) for all. Pieces of scotch tape should be pre-cut and attached to the rim of a hand basket for fast distribution along with the name tags in the other hand baskets.

MUSIC: "A-Tisket, A-Tasket," "Bingo," "Here We Go Round the Mulberry Bush," "Ida, Sweet as Apple Cider."

GREET SENIORS: One on one before the children enter.

RELAXING REHEARSAL: Review and sing "Ida, Sweet as Apple Cider" (music handout included.)

OPENING SONG: Choose your favorite.

MUSICAL WARM UP: In preparation for the next activity sing the adapted words (by Jane O'Brien) to "A-Tisket, A-Tasket."

> A-tisket, a-tasket, apples in my basket
> I'll give them to a special friend
> On the way, I'll share them.
> I'll share them, I'll share them,
> On my way I'll share them,
> I'll give them to a special friend
> And on my way I'll share them.

INTERACTIVE SONGS AND/OR ACTIVITIES:
Sharing: Announce that apples are regarded as the fruits of love to be shared with a friend. Ask everyone to sing the above song while the children pass out apple name tags to their grandfriends. Staff may need to help apply them to clothing with pre-cut scotch tape.

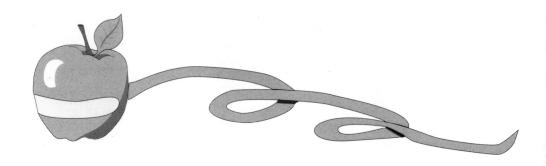

APPLES are A-PEELING

Discussion: Ways to prepare and eat apples. Adult can demonstrate peeling an apple with one continuous peel. Talk about apple cider, apple juice, applesauce, apple dumplings, apple butter and caramel apples and apple pie. Ask how these apple recipes are made. Encourage the child to ask their grandfriends for the answers.

Exercise: Pretend to make an apple pie to the tune of "Here We Go Round the Mulberry Bush." Leader can wear an apron and use a rolling pin.

1. Here we go round the apple tree, the apple tree, the apple tree,
   Here we go round the apple tree so early in the morning.
   (The children may join hands and circle around an adult pretending to be an apple tree with limbs extended.)
2. This is the way we pick the apples…(all reach up)
3. This is the way we roll out the crust…(both hands push forward, back)
4. This is the way we bake a pie…(push forward into the oven)
5. This is the way we eat the pie…(chew, smack lips)

Announce that an apple celebration will be held with a march to be followed by an apple treat.

MARCH/MOVEMENT: Distribute the rhythm sticks. March leader can wear the apron and lead with the rolling pin while adults sing "Ida, Sweet as Apple Cider" or "Don't Sit Under the Apple Tree" and children march around. Sticks can be deposited in a bushel basket at the end.

COOL DOWN: Teach and sing the adapted song to "Frere Jacques."

I love apples, I love apples,
In my tummy, in my tummy,
They're so good to eat, they're so good to eat,
Yum, yum, yummy, yum, yum, yummy.

Provide an apple treat for everyone. Apple slices, whole apples, or apple cookies

CLOSING MUSIC: Your favorite song you use regularly.

ANNOUNCEMENTS: Remind everyone of the old adage "An apple a day keeps the doctor away."

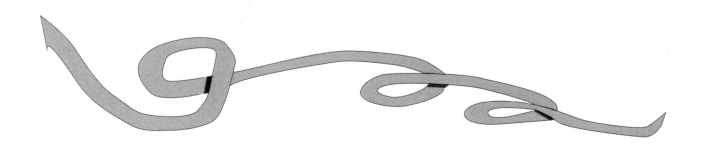

APPLES are A-PEELING

ADAPTATIONS FOR TWO-YEAR-OLDS

Interactive Songs and/or Activities: Exercise—children turn around individually rather than in circles.

Optional Activity: Use the felt board with pictures of various fruits. See Appendix A for felt patterns and directions.

RESOURCES:

All American Songbook
 "Don't Sit Under the Apple Tree" p. 20
Children's Songbook
 "The Mulberry Bush" p. 216
 "Frere Jacques" p. 234
Raffi Children's Favorites
 "Apples and Bananas" p. 14
Wee Sing and Play Musical Games
 "A-Tisket, A-Tasket" p. 30
1001 Jumbo Words and Music
 "Ida, Sweet as Apple Cider" p. 445

"WE MUST BRIDGE THE GAP OF YOUNG AND OLD BY ENCOURAGING ALTERNATE FORMS OF SOCIAL ORGANIZATION TO SUPPLEMENT THE FAMILY STRUCTURE FROM WHICH YOUNG AND OLD ARE OFTEN WITHDRAWN."
—*Patrick Ginnane*

A-PEELING BADGES

SPECIAL FRIEND

SPECIAL FRIEND

SPECIAL FRIEND

SPECIAL FRIEND

INTERGENERATIONAL SONG SHEET

Ida, Sweet as Apple Cider
(1903)

Words and music: Eddie Munson

Baseball for All

Program 3: BASEBALL

PREPARATION: Items needed include large inflatable plastic balls with one or two inflatable bats, popcorn or crackerjack treat (optional), baseball clothing for leader, paper baseball badge (pattern included) with clever name of your facility on it ("Day Care Darlings," for example), and scotch tape.

MUSIC: "Take Me Out to the Ball Game," "Enjoy Yourself, It's Later Than You Think," "In the Good Old Summer Time," "Bingo," "The Old Gray Mare," "Supercalifragilisticexpialidocious."

GREET SENIORS: One on one before children enter.

RELAXING REHEARSAL: Review the song "Take Me Out to the Ball Game".

OPENING SONG: Use the same song each session. Follow with an announcement of the theme and a few interviews asking "What do you like about baseball?" Prompt.

MUSICAL WARM UP: Ballplayers have to WARM UP with exercises. Have children stand while music plays and all do the appropriate actions.
"Enjoy Yourself..."— Rub hands together for pitching warm up.
"In The Good Old Summertime"— Practice throwing balls.
"B-I-N-G-O"— Practice batting balls.
"Take Me Out to the Ball Game"— Practice catching high and mid-level fly balls, and grounders.
"Supercalafragilisticexpialidocious"— Kids run in place as fast as possible, while seated adults pretend running with feet.
"The Old Gray Mare"— Chew gum (optional.)

INTERACTIVE SONGS AND/OR ACTIVITIES: Children and volunteers scotch tape the baseball badges on everyone. Children toss large balls to grandfriends and then back and forth while "Take Me out to the Ball Game" is playing in the background on tape or live piano. Select a person to come to bat. Have everyone yell "Play Ball!" Take turns at bat.

Baseball for All

MARCH/MOVEMENT: Pretend it's a stadium parade. Two choices of instruments to air play:
1. Trumpet—hold up hands in position and sing "toot, toot, toot"
2. Drums—beat an imaginary drum with sticks saying " drum, drum"

Music: "Hot Cross Buns"— strong beat.
"Twinkle, Twinkle Little Star"— these kids are baseball stars.

COOL DOWN: Kids sit and hear the seniors sing "Take Me Out to the Ball Game" and yell "One, two, three strikes, you're out!" in the middle of the song. Provide treat of peanuts or crackerjacks.

CLOSING MUSIC: Use the same song each session.

ANNOUNCEMENTS: Continue to practice those baseball exercises and songs.

ADAPTATIONS FOR TWO-YEAR-OLDS

Musical Warm Up: Practice throwing balls, pitching balls, catching balls, using the same music for "Take Me Out to the Ball Game." Then they can practice running in place to "Supercalifragilisticexpialidocious."

Interactive songs and/or activities: toss balls back and forth.
Use inflatable bat on floor for better coordination.

March/Movement: parade with only one imaginary instrument: drums or trumpet.

Cool Down: Practice showing one finger, then two, finally three. Grandfriends sing "Take Me Out to the Ball Game" Children shout,"One, Two, Three strikes. You're out!" and physically show the number of appropriate fingers. Ask grandfriends to be role models and do the same.

"HOW OLD WOULD YOU BE IF YOU DIDN'T KNOW HOW OLD YOU WAS?"
— *Satchel Paige, when asked the profound question of his age.*

BASEBALL FOR ALL

Play Ball!

RESOURCES:

Children's Songbook
  "B-I-N-G-O" p. 124
  "Hot Cross Buns" p. 224
  "Twinkle, Twinkle, Little Star" p. 202
Disney Collection
  "Supercalifragilisticexpialidocious" p. 118
Popular Songs That Live Forever
  "Take Me Out to the Ball Game" p. 222
Ultimate Fake Book
  "Old Gray Mare" p. 421
1001 Jumbo Words and Music
  "Enjoy Yourself, It's Later than You Think" p. 82
  "In the Good Old Summertime" p. 445

For additional ideas see *The Joy of Music in Maturity*
  "Take Me Out to the Ball Game" p. 239-243

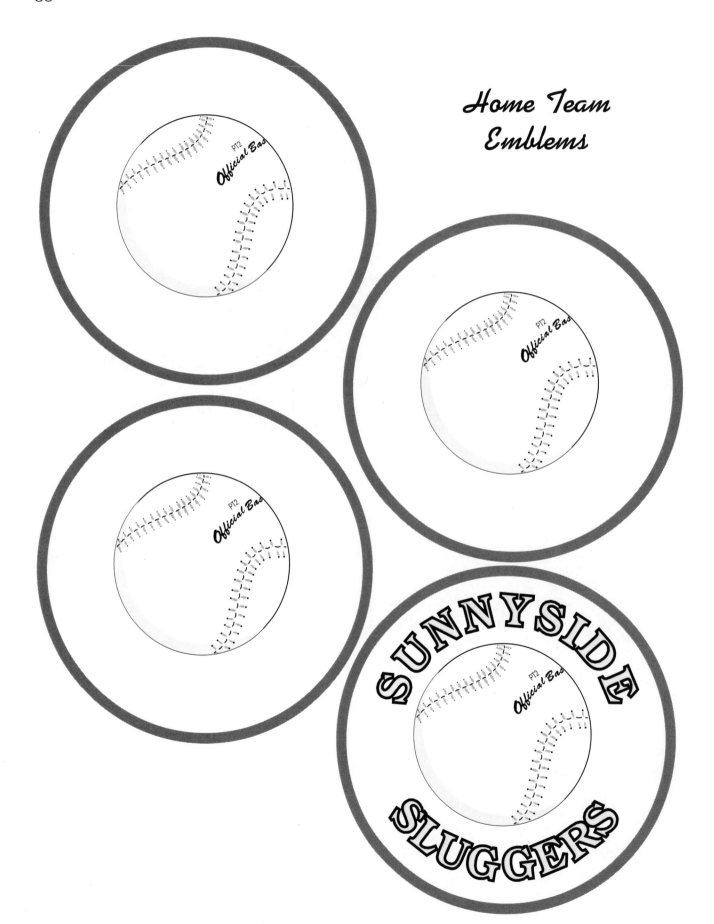

Home Team Emblems

ITS FOR THE BIRDS!!

Program 4: BIRDS

PREPARATION: Items include feathers for a child's back, pins to attach them. Fill plastic bird whistles with water by dipping in water filled bucket and place them on trays for easy distribution. (Keep paper towels handy for spills.) Five large letters of B-I-R-D-S should be pasted on separate posterboards.

MUSIC: "Let's All Sing Like the Birdies Sing," "Blue Danube Waltz," "Bye Bye Blackbird," "Blue Bird." and "Six Little Ducks."

GREET SENIORS: One on one before children enter.

RELAXING REHEARSAL: Practice "Let's All Sing Like the Birdies Sing" with the seniors. Remind them that they are helping the children learn a traditional old song. Also review "Six Little Ducks".

> Six little ducks that I once knew,
> fat ones, skinny ones, fair ones too.
> But the one little duck with the feather on his back,
> he (she) led the others with his "quack, quack, quack." (child's response)

Group imitates child's version with this chorus:

> Quack, quack, quack, quack, quack, quack
> He led the others with his quack, quack, quack.

> Down to the river they would go,
> wibble. wobble, wibble wobble, to and fro.
> But the one little duck with the feather on his back,
> he led the others with his "quack, quack, quack." (repeat chorus)

OPENING SONG: Your favorite. Discuss pet birds at home now or in the past. Invite everyone to make some bird sounds including whistling.

MUSICAL WARM UP: Lead a cheer: "Give me a B"—group yells "B." Continue until you spell B-I-R-D-S. End by asking "what does that spell?" Repeat with a child raising the letter called out.

IT'S FOR THE BIRDS!

"Six Little Ducks" activity: Pin a feather on a child who will be your lead duck. Group singing of "Six Little Ducks" with the chosen child leading their version of a quack. Group responds with the chorus. On the second verse have the child lead the "wibble wobble" with the children following his/her actions. Sing it all again with another child as the leader wearing the duck feathers or expand your leadership with two children.

INTERACTIVE SONGS AND/OR ACTIVITIES:
- Children pass out bird whistles filled with water.
- Have everyone blow and test their warblers.
- Grandfriends and leader sing "Let's All Sing Like the Birdies Sing" while everyone gets to respond with the bird whistles in the appropriate part of the song. Repeat.

    Let's all sing like the birdies sing, (tweet, tweet-tweet, tweet-tweet.)
    Let's all sing like the birdies sing, (sweet, sweet-sweet, sweet-sweet.)
    Let's all warble like nightingales, give your throat a treat,
    Take your tune from the birds, now you all know the words:
    (Tweet, tweet-tweet, tweet-tweet.)

- Play the "Blue Danube Waltz" on the piano or tape recorder and have everyone blow their whistle when you give the cues on the after beats (two and three.)
- Collect the bird whistles on the trays or in a pot. Water won't hurt anyone.

MARCH/MOVEMENT: Invite the children to fly like birds with wings flapping (arms outstretched) and bills tweeting as you play "Bye Bye Blackbird." Seniors can sing along with this old favorite or tweet and chirp.

COOL DOWN: Explain that you are going to adapt the tune of "Happy Birthday" to honor the birds today. Sing "Happy Bird Day to You." Point to various people in the room as you sing. Leader should circulate and use lots of eye contact.

CLOSING MUSIC: Your favorite.

ANNOUNCEMENTS: Keep your eyes and ears on the birds. BIrdwatching is a hobby now enjoyed by over one million Americans.

OPTIONAL ACTIVITY: Bring a live caged bird into the session for an experiment. Find out what music the bird prefers by listening for its response to the program. A child and an adult should judge.

IT'S FOR THE BIRDS!

ADAPTATIONS FOR TWO-YEAR-OLDS

Preparation: Items include bird whistles, blue, red and black caps. Music to "Blue Bird".

Musical Warm Up: Teach these words to "Mary Had a Little Lamb"
_____ (child's name) had a little bird, little bird, little bird
_____ had a little bird and it went tweet, tweet, tweet.

Interactive Songs and/or Activities: Pass out bird whistles filled with water. Let the children try them. Assist them if needed or replace with another whistle that works more easily. Use the above song "Mary Had a Little Bird."

Mary had a little bird, little bird, little bird,
Mary had a little bird and it went ____, ____, ____ (tweet, tweet tweet with bird whistles.)

Add other verses such as robin bird, big blackbird, cardinal, sparrow bird or cuckoo bird.

Sing the song "Blue Bird." Children take turns when the leader calls their name to be the bluebird and go in and out of the wheelchairs or seats of their grandfriends. Use flying arms.

Bluebird, bluebird, in and out the window,
Bluebird, bluebird, in and out the window,
Bluebird, bluebird, in and out the window,
Oh, _____ (name) is so happy.

Also use redbird, blackbird, and other birds. A blue, red or black hat should be worn as they fly in and out.

March/Movement: Birds (children) walk deliberately to the strong beat of the Bluebird song in a march tempo. Words can be changed.

Marching, marching for our grandfriends
Marching, marching for our grandfriends
Marching, marching for our grandfriends
Oh, _____(their name) is so happy.

"PERHAPS THIS IS THE MOST IMPORTANT FUNCTION OF MUSIC—TO GIVE WHOLENESS TO AN EVENT AND CONVEY A SHARED MOOD."
— *Margaret Mead*

IT'S FOR THE BIRDS!

RESOURCES:

Great Music's Greatest Hits
   "Blue Danube Waltz" p. 50
Raffi Children's Favorites
   "Six Little Ducks" p. 150
Real Little Best Fake Book Ever
   "Let's All Sing Like the Birdies Sing" p. 367
   "Bye, Bye Blackbird" p. 83
Wee Sing and Play Musical Games
   "Blue Bird" p. 26

For additional ideas see *The Joy of Music in Maturity*
   "Let's All Sing Like the Birdies Sing" program pp. 97-201

POSTERBOARD LETTERS

BIRDS

Enlarge these letters so that there is one letter per 8 ½ x 11" sheet.

Program 5: BIRTHDAYS

PREPARATION: Items needed include a birthday cake with appropriate number of candles (even if 100), match, wish wand (dowel with streamers and glittery star on top,) decorated chair for the celebrant, camera and a fake microphone (foam ball on a dowel.)

MUSIC: "Ring Around the Rosy," "Hot Cross Buns," "Mary Had a Little Lamb." March music, "Hail to the Chief"— music included on p. 46.

GREET SENIORS: One on one before the children enter.

RELAXING REHEARSAL: None.

OPENING SONG: Your favorite.

MUSICAL WARM UP: Ask the celebrant to take his/her specially decorated chair. Proclaim him/her Queen/King for a day. All sing to the tune of "Ring Around the Rosie"

    Happy, happy birthday,
    Happy, happy birthday,
    Happy Birthday Mr._____.

Adults sing one verse, children sing the second time and all join in the finale.

INTERACTIVE SONGS AND/OR ACTIVITIES:
Make a Wish Activity: Give the wish wand to the birthday person and have them hold it while you teach this song to the tune to "Hot Cross Buns"

    Make a wish, make a wish,
    You can tell it, you can yell it,
    Tell it now.

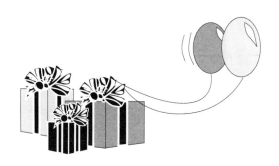

Happy Birthday!

After the celebrant tells their wish, they select the next person to do the same but only after the song is sung. Continue until all wishes are expressed. Let the celebrant keep the wish wand as a souvenir of this event. Photograph.

Light Birthday Cake: Bring out the birthday cake and light if permissible, even if you have to do it outdoors so the children can visualize the number of years this person has lived. Let the children pass out the cake to the grandfriends with the instructions of "don't eat it." Announce that the next humorous song will be to the tune of "Mary had a Little Lamb."

I've got birth-day cake in my hand, in my hand, in my hand,
I've got birth-day cake in my hand, I won-der what comes next.

Tell them that they can all take a bite and sing with their mouth full since there are no rules during this birthday party.

> I've got birthday cake in my mouth, in my mouth, in my mouth
> I've got birthday cake in my mouth, I wonder what comes next.

Everyone eats their cake and then looks around and sings:

> I've got birthday cake on the floor, on the floor, on the floor
> I've got birthday cake on the floor, I wonder what comes next.

Announce that this is the last verse to be sung with good feeling:

> I've got birthday spirit inside me, inside me, inside me,
> I've got birthday spirit inside me, it will last always.

MARCH/MOVEMENT: Distribute rhythm instruments and parade in front and behind celebrant. Dedicate this march to him/her. Play "Hail to the Chief" (p. 46) or any strong march music for this parade. Conclude by putting all instruments in one place and have everyone sit down.

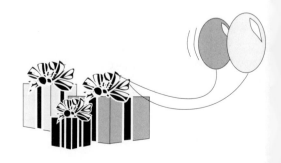

Happy Birthday!

COOL DOWN: Let the children realize the numerous years ahead of them and that their grandfriends have lived a long life full of experiences. Ask the grandfriends for advice to give these children as they face the years ahead. Use the fake microphone. Then ask the children to give advice to their grandfriends on what they feel is important to a happy day. Write the answers for your newsletter or post on a bulletin board.

CLOSING MUSIC: Your favorite.

ANNOUNCEMENTS: Remind everyone to look forward to their next birthday since it will be full of surprises—maybe even like this one.

OPTIONAL ACTIVITY: Paper flowers can be made or bought for use in corsages.

ADAPTATIONS FOR TWO-YEAR-OLDS

Interactive Songs and/or Activites: Eliminate the birthday cake eating song. Instead, two-year-olds can enjoy the cake and collect the plates. Children can go to their grandfriends and show them with their fingers how old they are. Grandfriends can assist if necessary. Omit asking grandfriends for advice.

Cool Down: Replace with the children telling about any birthday party they remember. It could be theirs, a friend's or an adult's.

Sharing 100 years

> "Being with these children is better than medicine."
>
> — John, age 100

RESOURCES:

Wee Sing America
   March music for piano
Wee Sing Children's Songs
   "Ring Around the Rosy" p. 41
Wee Sing Nursery Rhymes
   "Hot Cross Buns" p. 30
   "Mary Had a Little Lamb" p. 12

MARCH MUSIC

Hail To The Chief
(1812)

Music: James Sanderson

Program 6:
CHINESE NEW YEAR

PREPARATION: Items needed include long red paper or cloth streamers for all (red represents good luck), Chinese paper lanterns (pattern included), to be put on a stick for march time, Chinese New Year's dragon for children (pattern included), picture or stuffed animal to represent the zodiac sign (check your library for the current year data, as it falls between mid January and early March), rhythm instruments—especially sticks, and fortune cookies.

MUSIC: "Happy Birthday," "A-Tisket A-Tasket," "Chinatown, My Chinatown."

GREET SENIORS: One on one before the children enter.

RELAXING REHEARSAL: Inform the adults that the celebration of a Chinese New Year represents a new beginning for all so this session will be like a birthday for everyone. It also symbolizes the end of winter and the beginning of spring. It presents the opportunity to celebrate good things ahead. Sing the adapted words to "A-Tisket A-Tasket" as follows:

> A dragon, a dragon
> See the tail a-waggin'
> The girls and boys
> All bring us joy
> Here's our Chinese dragon.

OPENING SONG: Your customary favorite.

MUSICAL WARM UP: Announce the theme of celebrating the Chinese New Year as mentioned above. Sing "Happy Birthday to You," (point to everyone) then to "Me" (point to self) and then to "Us" (arms raised upwards). Explain to the children that many people from China live in the U.S. and this is a birthday celebration following some of their traditions. Then using the same tune sing "Happy Chinese New Year" (repeat line one) then "It's the year of the _____" (zodiac sign), ending with the first line.

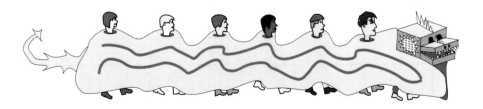

Happy Chinese New Year!

INTERACTIVE SONGS AND/OR ACTIVITIES:
- Exercise with red streamers distributed to all. Use large sweeping motions to represent house cleaning. Music of "Chinatown, My Chinatown."
- Repeat using streamers stretching up and down. (spreading good luck)
- Urge everyone to observe the colors and motions of others. Collect.

MARCH/MOVEMENT: Pass out instruments to those not in the parade. Place children in the dragon. In China, dragons are a symbol of goodness and strength, not evil. Use the lanterns for decoration or for the adults to wave to the tempo of the music. All participate joyously with instruments and sing the "Dragon Song" many times. Dragon should go among the grandfriends.

COOL DOWN: Collect all props and instruments. When everyone is seated pass out fortune cookies. Share the best thoughts. Discuss the good things that might happen to people this coming year.

CLOSING MUSIC: Your favorite.

ANNOUNCEMENTS: You announce that your Chinese fortune predicted one of the following:

- You will look in the mirror and see a wonderful person.
- Tonight you will dream of your favorite place.

OPTIONAL ACTIVITY: Fish kites for decoration or parade waving.

Our Dragon

"My favorite excuse to leave my desk is to be a part of the intergenerational music program."

— Sharon, administrator
(age not revealed)

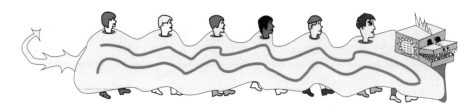

Happy Chinese New Year!

> **ADAPTATIONS FOR TWO-YEAR-OLDS**
>
> **Preparation:** Paste a dragon picture on a tongue depressor for kids. (See instructions.)
>
> **Interactive Songs and/or Activities:** Use only one.
>
> **March/Movement:** Children parade with paper dragon to replace parade dragon.

DRAGON INSTRUCTIONS FOR TWO YEAR OLDS

1. Copy the pattern below with enlargement, if available.
2. Cut out, color, fold on dashed line and paste onto tongue depressor.

RESOURCES:

Children's Songbook
   "Happy Birthday to You" p. 252
   "A-Tisket A-Tasket" p. 110 tune for
     "Dragon Song"

Real Little Best Fake Book
   "Chinatown, My Chinatown" p.111

Happy Chinese New Year!

CHINESE LANTERN INSTRUCTIONS:

1. Fold a brightly colored 8½ x 11" sheet of construction paper in half in the 11" dimension.

2. Make cuts starting from the fold at ¾" intervals to within ¾" of the opposite edge.

3. Unfold and make a circle with each of the uncut edge strips. Secure with tape.

4. Cut a 12" length of string and attach to opposite sides of one end as a hanger.

5. Optional: Add ¾ x 11" strips of another color to top and bottom for reinforcement and interest.

PARADE DRAGON INSTRUCTIONS:

1. Procure two cardboard boxes of roughly 14" dimensions for the dragon's head. One dimension of the two needs to be the same.

2. Cut one box into shallow trays for the jaws. One edge of each (the one which will be inside the other box) can be cut off to allow better visibility from within the head. Line the edges of these trays with teeth cut from white paper.

3. Cut off the back and half of the front of the other box for use as the main head.

4. Glue the jaws into this head.

5. Add eyes, nostrils and decorations of paper, markers or paints.

6. Obtain a piece of cloth (perhaps from old sheets) of 44" width and length sufficient to cover youngsters when they're in a comfortable lineup.

7. Cut an X with 4" arms at points along the centerline of the cloth separated by 14"

8. Decorate the sides with dragon-like stripes and scales and Chinese symbols, making the two side panels roughly the same.

9. Staple the front end to the box and close the rear end by stapling it shut and including into it a cardboard dragon tail. Be sure that no staple points are exposed.

10. Bring the dragon to life by having each child put his or her head through one of the X openings. The "tough" guy of the class should hold up the head and lead the dragon parade while looking out through the jaws.

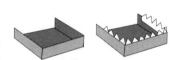
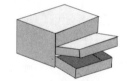

STEP RIGHT UP!

Program 7: CIRCUS

PREPARATION: Make clown hats for the children ahead of program (pattern included) and several larger hats for any adults desiring one. Decorate the room by hanging streamers from a central point radiating out to a big circle to form the circus arena.

Use colorful tape to form a large circus ring or use a large blanket. Grandfriends should sit around the circus ring in rows. Hang colorful balloons. Advertise with posters saying "Ringling Brothers, Barnum, Bailey, _____ Circus" (name of your facility.) Invite children to bring stuffed circus animals such as horses, lions, tigers, monkeys, elephants and dogs. Make long six foot crepe paper streamers and attach to dowels for the children. Ask everyone to wear bright colors. Staff could wear circus side show costumes. Leader should wear a ringmaster outfit of top hat, big bow tie, suit, gloves and baton. Taste treat of popcorn or cotton candy optional.

MUSIC: "The More We Get Together," "There Is a Funny Clown," "Daring Young Man (on the Flying Trapeze)," any Sousa march, "Blue Danube Waltz," and "Jumbo Elephant" to the tune of "Row, Row, Row Your Boat" and "Farmer in the Dell."

GREET SENIORS: One on one before the children enter.

RELAXING REHEARSAL: Organize a singing calliope with three sections of adult singers including the staff. Parts can be sung or spoken.

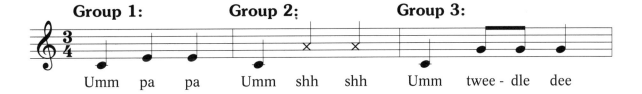

Those not in the calliope section should sing "The More We Get Together" along with the calliope accompaniment. The first downbeat or "ummm" comes on the word "More" after the group sings the upbeat word "The." For added fun sing this standing up. On beat one, lower self, then stand for beats two and three. Repeat.

STEP RIGHT UP!

Rehearse the "Funny Clown" song. Use the tune from "The Farmer in the Dell."

There is a funny clown,
_____is his (her) name
and she (he) will do tricks for you,
for our circus game.

OPENING SONG: Ringmaster leads children into the arena while taped circus music is playing in the background, A decorated wagon carrying all the toy animals is optional, otherwise the children carry them. Use your traditional opening song.

MUSICAL WARM UP: All sing "The More We Get Together" with the optional calliope accompaniment. Children can move their animals to the beat of the music.

INTERACTIVE SONGS AND/OR ACTIVITIES:

Part one: The ringmaster announces the opening of the circus. Children pass out streamers on a stick to their grandfriends and keep one for themselves. The children lead the exercise with their streamers creating colors and patterns that are very artistic.

- Move streamers in large circles to "The Daring Young Man (on the Flying Trapeze.)"
- Move streamers up and down to any Sousa march. Example: "Stars and Stripes Forever."
- Now make a figure eight to any waltz. Example: "Blue Danube."
- Ringmaster announces that the Clown Act is next after all the streamers are collected for another circus event.

Part two: While children sit in a large circle, teach the adapted song "There is a Funny Clown." Give each child a chance to do a funny trick. They can ask a grandfriend for a suggestion. Ringmaster announces that the next event is the elephants on parade.

Part three: The leader sings "The Jumbo Elephant" while children walk like elephants around the ring. One arm should sway like their trunk, the other should be behind them as a wagging tail. Bending over, swing trunk from side to side slowly to the music. The music should be repeated several times along with actions.

STEP RIGHT UP!

Use the adapted words to "Row, Row, Row Your Boat" as follows:

>Jumbo elephant
>You have the longest nose
>It reaches up in the air
>Then down to your toes.

The ringmaster announces that the next event is the gala parade.

MARCH/MOVEMENT: Using taped circus music, have the children pick up their stuffed animals and any other props they brought, and parade around the room several times. The adults should clap to the music acknowledging the joy of the children. Children can march out of the room or enjoy a cool down session.

COOL DOWN: Everyone seated gets a treat of popcorn or cotton candy as circus music is played softly.

CLOSNG MUSIC: Your favorite that you use regularly.

ANNOUNCEMENTS: Close your eyes anytime and recall the colorful sights and merry sounds of the circus performed today with all the generations involved.

OPTIONAL ACTIVITY: The interactive activity could be animal charades. Grandfriend and child decide on which animal the child will represent and act like in the ring. Everyone then tries to guess the animal.

> ### ADAPTATIONS FOR TWO-YEAR-OLDS
> **Musical Warm Up:** Eliminate the calliope.
>
> **Interactive Activity:** Use only one free movement with the streamers. Encourage the children to share any circus memories
>
> **Optional:** Ride their hobby horses around the ring.

STEP RIGHT UP!

RESOURCES:

Legit Fake Book
    "Blue Danube Waltz" p. 410
    "Farmer in the Dell" p. 96
    "The Daring Young Man (on the Flying Trapeze)" p. 229
    "Stars and Stripes Forever" (Sousa march) p. 450
    "Row, Row, Row Your Boat" p. 293

Circus compact disc or tape
    Under the Big Top Angel CDC 0777 7 54728 2 0
    Great American Main Street Band

CLOWN HAT DIRECTIONS:

1. Cut the general pattern at right from an 8½" x 11" page for a small 3½" diameter hat or from an 11" x 17" sheet for the adult hats of 5½" diameter. Decorate with stickers, stars, or crayon. Leave a ½" opening in the top.

2. Cut eight 6" x 10" strips of colorful newspaper sections. Staple along one of the 10" sides. Fringe the other side. Cut this into two 5" pieces for two hats. Roll one of these up, put into the top of the hat and secure with a staple.

   Optional: Staple a pipe cleaner coming out of the top. To the top end of the pipe cleaner staple or glue a colorful flower formed from a cupcake paper cup cut to the bottom crease or from construction paper.

3. Staple or tape ribbon to the sides of the hat to tie under the chin.

DOLLS are DIFFERENT

Program 8: DOLLS

PREPARATION: Prepare a letter to parents asking that the children bring one of their dolls (not a stuffed animal) for the next session. (Sample in Appendix E) Invite grandfriends, with a letter or poster, to bring a doll or borrow one from their relatives. Collect extra dolls such as Raggedy Ann and Andy, Kewpie Dolls, Storybook doll, Dydee Doll and others. Collect younger dolls such as Barbie and Ken. Songsheet "Oh, You Beautiful Doll" (included.)

MUSIC: "Oh, You Beautiful Doll," "March of the Toys," "Hello Dolly."

GREET SENIORS: One on one before children enter.

RELAXING REHEARSAL: Pass out the large print song sheets (enclosed) and sing "Oh, You Beautiful Doll." The children about to enter are "living dolls."

OPENING SONG: Use the same song each session.

MUSICAL WARM UP: Sing the adapted song "If You're Happy and You Know It!"

>If you're happy and you know it, raise your doll.
>If you're happy and you know it, raise your doll.
>If you're happy and you know it,
>then your face will surely show it!
>If you're happy and you know it raise your doll.

(Raise up high for all to see.)

Additional verses and corresponding exercises Rock your doll, bounce your doll, hug your doll

INTERACTIVE SONGS AND/OR ACTIVITES: Sing one more time using the words "share your doll." Children should take their dolls to their grandfriends and exchange memories. Soft music in the background could be "Hello Dolly," or "Oh, You Beautiful Doll." Everyone is welcome to use the microphone and tell about their doll. Prompts sometimes necessary.

DOLLS are DIFFERENT

Aim for the following conversations:
- Construction of old dolls—china faces, clothing, rag dolls
- Construction of new dolls—plastic parts, sound activated, names
- Promote contrasting the differences and similarities
- Talk about the popularity of Barbie and Ken Dolls
- Ask about gender dolls
- Discuss ethnic dolls
- Ponder what makes a doll your favorite

Grandfriends should sing "Oh, You Beautiful Doll" for the children. It was written in 1911 and like some dolls, has become a favorite.

Discussion: Leader should introduce by singing the following song with adapted words to "Oh Where, Oh Where, Has My Little Dog Gone":

> Oh where, oh where has my dolly gone? (Power Ranger, Barbie)
> Oh where, oh where can she be?
> The table is set, the cookies are done,
> Tell her it's time for tea.

Both generations should talk about tea parties for their dolls. Compare foods served years ago and what children serve today. Ask the boys if they would like to go to a tea party.

MARCH/MOVEMENT: All dolls should be set aside so the dolls can "watch" the children march with their rhythm band instruments. Distribute instruments and march to the "March of the Toys."

COOL DOWN: Everyone should be seated for an open discussion of the topic "If you could be a doll, which one would you like to be?"

CLOSING MUSIC: Use the same song each session.

ANNOUNCEMENTS: Distribute song sheets of "Oh You Beautiful Doll" for all to take as a reminder of today's program as well as a promotion of renewing old music.

OPTIONAL ACTIVITY: Cut out a series of paper dolls with hands joining. (pattern included) Decorate the room with them or have individual names on each one.

DOLLS are DIFFERENT

> **ADAPTATIONS FOR TWO-YEAR-OLDS**
>
> **Preparation:** Low table, tablecloth, tea set, beverage and snack.
>
> **Interactive songs and/or activities:** Consider having a tea party for the dolls using a small, low table and the above suggestions. Ask if they would like to invite a grandfriend to the party or deliver a snack to them.

RESOURCES:

Children's Songbook
   "If You're Happy and You Know It" p. 176
Great Music's Greatest Hits
   "March of the Toys" p. 155
Legal Fake Book
   "Oh You Beautiful Doll" p. 212
Treasury of Best Loved Songs
   "Hello, Dolly" p. 60
Wee Sing Nursery Rhymes and Lullabies
   "Oh Where, Oh Where Has My Little Dog Gone?" p. 38

For additional ideas see *The Joy of Music in Maturity*
   "Oh, You Beautiful Doll" program p. 299-303

"Why don't they make Grandpa Dolls?"
— Alex, age 3½

INTERGENERATIONAL SONG SHEET

Oh! You Beautiful Doll
(1911)

Words: A. Seymour Brown
Music: Nat D. Ayer

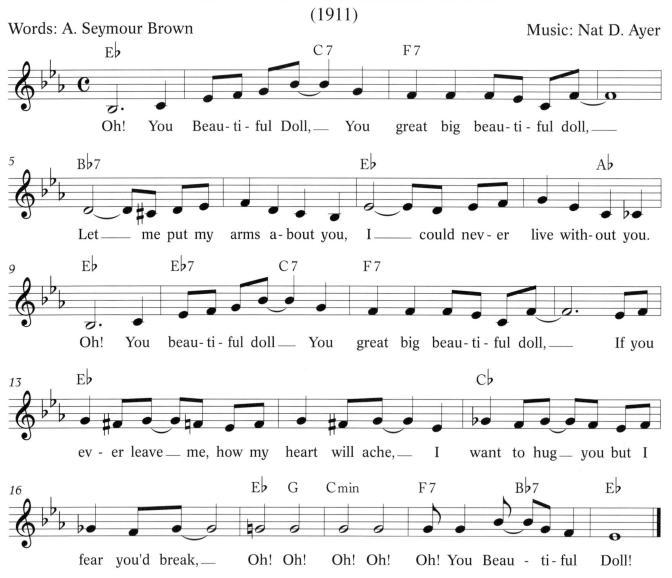

Oh! You Beau-ti-ful Doll, You great big beau-ti-ful doll, Let me put my arms a-bout you, I could nev-er live with-out you. Oh! You beau-ti-ful doll You great big beau-ti-ful doll, If you ev-er leave me, how my heart will ache, I want to hug you but I fear you'd break, Oh! Oh! Oh! Oh! Oh! You Beau-ti-ful Doll!

Paper Doll Chain Pattern

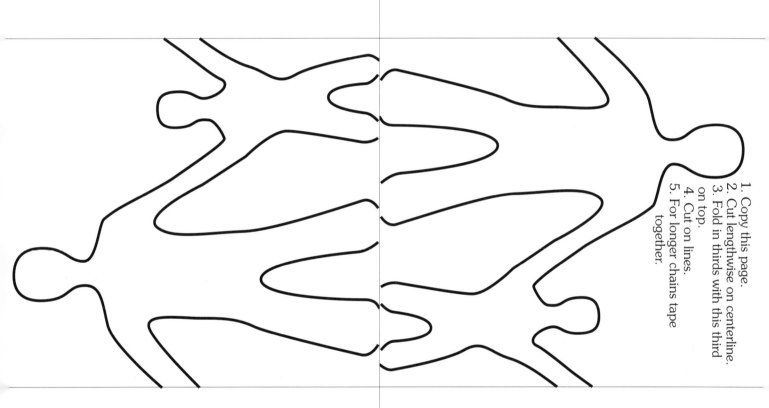

1. Copy this page.
2. Cut lengthwise on centerline.
3. Fold in thirds with this third on top.
4. Cut on lines.
5. For longer chains tape together.

Autumn Calling

Program 9: FALL

PREPARATION: Items needed include paper plates with 3 types of local leaves pasted on them, fall leaves in a basket, (northern friends can mail them to you) or paper leaves, rake, leaf blower, and a compost bag.

MUSIC: "Autumn Calling" (music handout.) Music for "Hey Diddle, Diddle," "In the Shade of the Old Apple Tree," "Shine On Harvest Moon," "Here We Go Round the Mulberry Bush" and "Brahms' Lullaby."

GREET SENIORS: One on one before children enter.

RELAXING REHEARSAL: Teach seniors "Autumn Calling" to the tune of "Frere Jacques."

OPENING SONG: Your favorite song that you use consistently.

MUSICAL WARM UP: Pass out leaf plates to children only. Seniors sing "Autumn calling." Children hold plates up high, gentle fall down with them. Repeat for more merriment.

INTERACTIVE SONGS AND/OR ACTIVITIES:
- Children pass out additional plates to grandfriends.
- Take a poll of who has similar leaves (everyone with a maple leaf, raise it high.) Children run up to one that matches theirs.
- Exercise with plates by following a leader: The Leader has everyone count down 8, 7, 6, 5, 4, 3, 2, 1 to set tempo. Keep to a count of eight beats before changing plate tap.
   "In the Shade of the Old Apple Tree"—Thump the plate on your thigh, head, and knee. Announce change in tempo and continue as above with a new leader of any age.
   "Hey Diddle Diddle"— Ask for a child volunteer to lead the activity.
- Leaf shower—The leader stands in center. At the count of three everyone gets to shower her/him with their leaf plate. Children get to pick them up.

AUTUMN CALLING

Leaf raking activity: Dump leaves on floor and have everyone sing and do the motions to the adapted "Here We Go Round the Mulberry Bush" song.

> This is the way we raked the leaves, raked the leaves, raked the leaves
> This is the way we raked the leaves, long, long ago.

Discuss raking, burning, smelling, of the leaves in the past. Talk about the changes in burning bans, composting, leaf blowers. Sing about these changes and do the motions for exercise.

> This is the way we jumped in the leaves…(Kids jump, adults lift feet)
> Now we have to bag our leaves…(Lifting motions, stuffing bags)
> Now we have to blow our leaves…(Both hands on handle and move a lot)

MARCH/MOVEMENT: Children should take two plates and clap them together as they march to "Shine on Harvest Moon." Seniors should provide rhythmic clapping or sing this old song.

COOL DOWN: Leaves should be vacuumed or bagged. A basket should be available to hold the leaf plates. Other options are to collect them or use them as souvenirs.

Ask everyone to pretend they are lying in a pile of autumn leaves. Children can lie down and relax on the floor. Let the grandfriends reminisce with fond memories of this activity. Recommend it to the children as a great way to relax and enjoy autumn. On the piano softly play "Brahms Lullaby."

CLOSING MUSIC: Your favorite.

ANNOUNCEMENTS: Distribute music for everyone's collection.

"IF THE FUTURE IS TO BE REALLY ACCEPTED, IT MUST BE ANCHORED
IN A FEELING FOR THE PAST."
— Margaret Mead

AUTUMN CALLING

ADAPTATIONS FOR TWO-YEAR-OLDS

Preparation: Cut out red, yellow, green and brown paper or felt leaves.

Music: "Falling Leaves," (music handout), "Frere Jacques," tape of "Turkey in the Straw."

Musical Warm Up: Pass out felt leaves to children only, discuss and locate colors.

Leader sings to the tune of "Frere Jacques"
   Who has the yellow leaf, who has the yellow leaf?
     _____ (child's name) does, _____ does.
     _____ has the yellow leaf, _____ has the yellow leaf
   She's so smart, she's so smart.

Interactive Songs and/or Activitites: Have children pass out felt leaves to grandfriends. Assist with placement of leaves on seniors upper clothing if necessary. Leader sings "Falling Leaves" song. Once familiar have everyone sing it. Repeat with a strong emphasis on the colors. Sing verse one as printed. On verse two, have the children fall down.

March/Movement: Children march to music of "Turkey in the Straw" (tape.)

RESOURCES:

Children's Songbook
   "Here We Go Round the Mulberry Bush" p. 216
   "Hey, Diddle Diddle" p. 226
Popular Song's That Live Forever
   "Shine On Harvest Moon" p. 228
Wee sing Nursery Rhymes and Lullabies
   "Brahms' Lullaby" p. 58
1001 Jumbo Words and Music
   "In the Shade of the Old Apple Tree" p. 444
   "Turkey in the Straw" p. 555

For additional ideas see *The Joy of Music in Maturity*
   "Praise for Autumn" p. 400-404
   "Praise for the Harvest" 405-409

AUTUMN LEAVES

64

INTERGENERATIONAL SONG SHEET

Autumn Calling

(to the melody of "Frére Jacques")

Words: J. Shaw   Music: French Folk Song

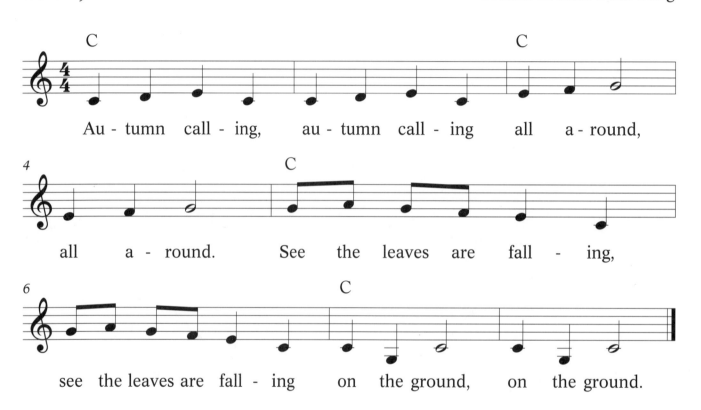

INTERGENERATIONAL SONG SHEET

Falling Leaves

Words and Music: J. Shaw

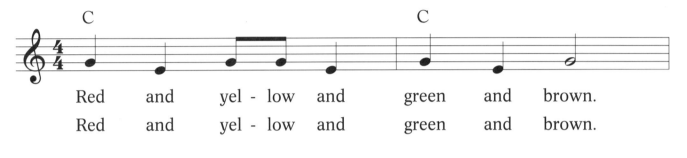

Red and yel - low and green and brown.
Red and yel - low and green and brown.

See the leaves come fall - ing down.
Now the kids come fall - ing down.

Baby, It's You

Program 10: FAMILY

PREPARATION: Invite family members in advance, especially baby brothers and sisters, to attend the session. Bring along everyone's personal baby picture with their name on the backside. Display program announcement and invitation on bulletin boards or posters. Items needed include a polaroid camera, a few mystery photos of famous people, cartoon characters, baby dinosaur, and a live baby. Also bring a doll cradle or doll swing and dress up clothes for the children: lots of hats, ties, beads, purses, clothing.

MUSIC: "I Love You," "He's Got the Whole World in His Hands," "Baby Face," "Frere Jacques," and other lullabies of your choice.

GREET SENIORS: One on one before the children enter.

RELAXING REHEARSAL: Review favorite lullabies and songs about babies: "Rock-a-Bye Baby," "Brahms' Lullaby," "Too-ra-loo-ra-loo-ral, that's an Irish Lullaby," "Hush Little, Baby," "All Night, All Day," "Sleep, Baby, Sleep," "Pretty Baby," "Baby Face," "You Must Have Been a Beautiful Baby."

OPENING SONG: Welcome all the families with your favorite opening song.

MUSICAL WARM UP:
- Then all sing "He's Got the Whole World in His Hands" with actions.

   He's got the itsy, bitsy babies in his hands…(Rock "baby" in your arms.)
   He's got all the visitors…(Everyone points to all the newcomers.)
   He's got all the mommies…(Let just the mommies sing this verse.)
   He's got all the daddies…(Dad's turn to sing.)
   He's got all the children…(Encourage loud voices.)
   He's got all the grandfriends…(Sing with joy to celebrate longevity.)
   He's got everybody…(Point to as many as possible.)

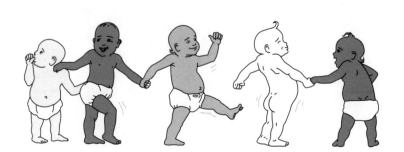

Baby, It's You

- Then sing the endearing "I Love You" song that Barney the dinosaur promotes.

  I love you, you love me (point)
  We're a happy family (big smiles)
  With a great big hug (hug self)
  And a kiss from me to you (throw a kiss)
  Won't you say you love me too?

"I Love You" Lyrics by Lee Bernstein
©1983 Simbarah Music, a division of The Lyons Group. Used with Permission.

INTERACTIVE SONGS AND/OR ACTIVITES:
Picture sharing: Open this activity with a solo or group singing of "Baby Face" or "Pretty Baby." Remind everyone that they were all babies once. Return photos to everyone and then ask them to share their pictures. Encourage the children to see as many grandfriends pictures as possible. Softly play or provide the music for "Baby Face" in the background.

Mystery photo: Children are seated. Bring out a few large mystery photos and guess their identity.

MARCH/MOVEMENT: Children dress up like mommy and daddy with the props suggested and march to "Baby Face" and "The Mickey Mouse March." Return all props.

COOL DOWN: Talk about favorite lullabies that were once sung. Interview several adults. Choose one lullaby for the group to sing. Take a poll showing regional differences. If a baby is available, all sing his or her favorite lullaby. Slowly and quietly sing to this dear child.

CLOSING MUSIC: Close with heartfelt thanks to all who attended this family session. Sing your traditional closing song.

ANNOUNCEMENTS: Give thanks for the opportunities that babyhood provides and be glad to eat your vegetables so you'll continue to live a long time.

OPTIONAL ACTIVITY: Children can introduce their family members on the fake or real microphone. If shy, let an adult introduce the child.

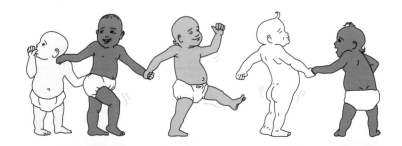

Baby, It's You

> **ADAPTATIONS FOR TWO-YEAR-OLDS**
>
> **Musical Warm Up:** Replace song with the following words to the melody of "Frere Jacques." Sing about daddy, baby, grandma, grandpa too.
>
> I love mommy, I love mommy,
> Yes, I do, Yes, I do,
> And my mommy loves me,
> And my mommy loves me,
> Loves me too, loves me too.
>
> Play pat-a-cake with the grandfriends.

RESOURCES:

Children's Songbook
　"Frere Jacques" p. 234
Disney Collection
　"Mickey Mouse March" p. 82
Family Songbook
　"Pretty Baby" p. 28
Family Songbook of Faith and Joy
　"He's Got the Whole World
　　in His Hands" p. 226
Popular Songs That Live Forever
　"Baby Face" p. 110
Raffi Children's Favorites
　"This Old Man" p. 156
　　(tune for "I Love You")
Wee Sing Nursery Rhymes and Lullabies
　Good collection of lullaby songs

Going to our Grandfriends

"My new grandfriend likes to pinch my cheeks a lot!"
— Caitlin, age 4

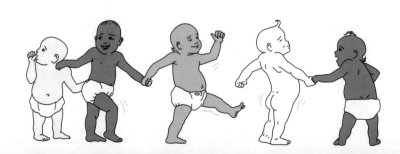

OUR FLAG FOREVER

Program 11: OUR FLAG

PREPARATION: Bring small and large newspaper hats (pattern provided), small flags for all (purchased), red, white and blue 2-inch ribbons of cloth or crepe paper (12' length), baskets for ribbons, large flag for leader, handout for "Three Cheers for the Red, White and Blue" (provided.)

MUSIC: "You're a Grand Old Flag," "Stars and Stripes Forever," "Yankee Doodle" and "Three Cheers for the Red, White and Blue" music handout to give everyone as a momento of today's program.

GREET SENIORS: One on one before the children enter.

RELAXING REHEARSAL: Review "Three Cheers for the Red, White and Blue" (originally "Columbia the Gem of the Ocean" as composed in 1843.) Rehearse only the chorus section provided below.

OPENING SONG:
Your favorite.

MUSICAL WARM UP:
Honor the flag by telling the story of how it was first made in 1777, perhaps by Betsy Ross, with 13 stars representing the first states of the U.S.A. Explain that now there are many more states with a star for each but that the 13 stripes stand for the original states. Invite the children to count the stripes and the stars out loud. If help is needed, ask the grandfriends to assist in counting out loud as a group. Teach the song "Three Cheers for the Red, White and Blue" (music handout.)

We Pledge Allegiance

"Sometimes they use bad words like when they talk about politics."

— Mark, age 5

OUR FLAG FOREVER

INTERACTIVE SONGS AND/OR ACTIVITY: Children pass out red, white and blue ribbons in sections. Leader sings a solo or plays a tape of the chorus only. Ask for a visible leader for each colored section. Sing slowly and as the color is mentioned, raise your ribbon up high. End with all ribbons raised and shaking joyously. Repeat after first rehearsal. Children should collect the ribbons in baskets.

MARCH/MOVEMENT: Pass out paper hats to all the children. Children should ask the seniors if they would like one in a larger size. Distribute flags to everyone and invite them to a flag parade. Leader should carry a larger flag. Parade with the following music on piano or tape:

"Yankee Doodle"
"Stars and Stripes Forever"
"Three Cheers for the Red, White and Blue "

COOL DOWN: Children should be seated and all should slowly wave their flags to the music of "You're a Grand Old Flag." Reflect on the words as you watch your flag waving. Collect flags and hats or invite anyone to keep theirs as a momento of the flag celebration.

CLOSING MUSIC: Your favorite.

ANNOUNCEMENTS: Remind everyone to be proud of the flag and keep on singing about it.

> ### ADAPTATIONS FOR TWO-YEAR-OLDS
>
> **Interactive Song and/or activity:** Use tri-colored crepe paper instead of individual colors. Sing "Three Cheers for the Red, White and Blue," raising the paper on all stanzas. This makes a good souvenir to keep as a reminder of the colors of America and the good times today. Sing "Twinkle, Twinkle Little Star" together.
>
> - Two-year-olds find it easier to point to the stars on the flag while the adults count them out loud.
>
> - Ask the children to locate the colors of red, white and blue on the flag. Then ask them to find a grandfriend wearing the same color.

OUR FLAG FOREVER

RESOURCES:

Wee Sing America
"Yankee Doodle" p. 22
"Three Cheers for the Red, White and Blue" p. 11
"Stars and Stripes Forever" p. 12
"You 're a Grand Old Flag" p. 10

For additional ideas see *The Joy of Music in Maturity*
"It's a Grand Old Flag" program p. 245-249
"Go Forth on the Fourth of July" parade p. 279-284

Generations on Parade

NEWSPAPER HAT INSTRUCTIONS:

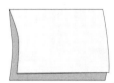

1. Start with a double sheet of newspaper.
   (Tabloid size works best for the children's hats.)

2. Starting from the closed corners, fold down until the two corners meet. Crease flat.

3. Fold up the strips which show at the bottom, one to each side. Be sure to catch the corner folds of step 2 with one of these strips.

4. Spread the center apart and set it on an eager head.

Proud Americans

INTERGENERATIONAL SONG SHEET

Three Cheers for the Red, White and Blue

(From the song "Columbia, the Gem of the Ocean")

Words: Thomas A. Becket   Music: David Shaw

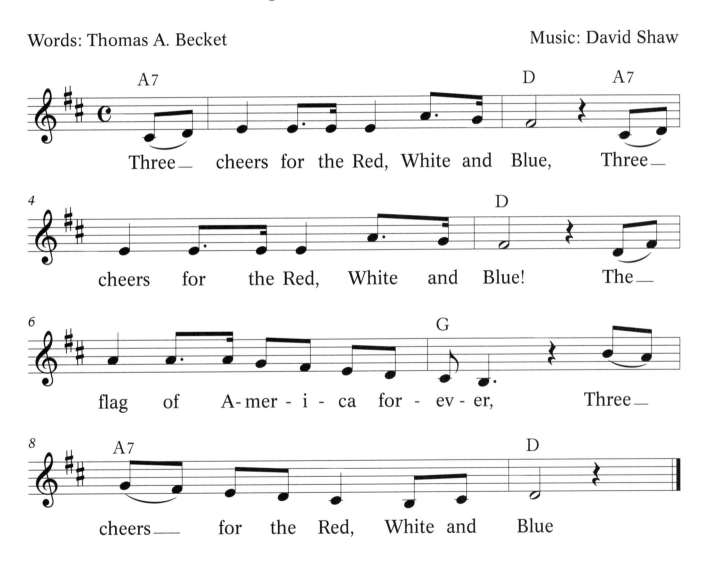

FLYING HIGH

Program 12: FLYING

PREPARATION: Items needed include 5 attached helium balloons on strings, paper airplanes for all, (pattern included). Large toy airplane for a prop.

MUSIC: "Daring Young Man (on the Flying Trapeze)," "Army Air Corps Song," You're a Grand Old Flag," "I'm Forever Blowing Bubbles," " Let's All Sing Like the Birdies Sing," "Rudolph the Red Nosed Reindeer," "Angels We have Heard on High," "Come Josephine in my Flying Machine," "Old MacDonald Had a Farm."

GREET SENIORS: One on one before children enter.

RELAXING REHEARSAL: Teach this flying song to the tune of "Old MacDonald had a Farm"

"Old MacDonald had a plane, hip, hip, hip, hurrah
and on this plane he had a _____(name a part)"

Help children later on with this.

OPENING SONG: Your favorite.

MUSICAL WARM UP: Ask, "What flies?" (Kites, bubbles, airplanes, flies, angels, flag, birds, trapeze artists, balloons, Rudolph the reindeer, ghosts, and time.) Discuss.

Preparation for takeoff: Sway to the music of "Daring Young Man (on the Flying Trapeze)" (movement) Teach "Flying song" (Old MacDonald) as final step for "takeoff." Use the airplane prop and have someone point out the part you are singing about:

"On this plane he had a _____" (wing, tail, nose, pilot, seat)

INTERACTIVE SONGS AND/OR ACTIVITY: Children pass out paper airplanes and keep one. Line children up—facing helium balloon bouquet. Sing the "Flying Song" using the verse "and on this plane he had a pilot" as everyone flies their paper plane. At the end have one child count down to "blast-off." Fire away.

FLYING HIGH

Children pick up planes and redistribute. Repeat activity. If a balcony is available, take the kids upstairs and let the planes soar. Have the children interview the adults with the question, "Have you every been in an airplane? Hot air balloon? Where? How was it?" Come back to the microphone and give report.

MARCH/MOVEMENT: March with airplanes in hand to the music of the "Army Air Corps Song."

COOL DOWN: A musical quiz of old time songs with clues of things that fly. Children either seated or asking their grandfriends for the answers.

"It's a Grand Old Flag"
"The Daring Young Man (on the Flying Trapeze)"
"I'm Forever Blowing Bubbles"
"Let's All Sing like the Birdies Sing"
"Rudolph the Red Nosed Reindeer"
"Angels We have Heard on High"
"Come Josephine in My Flying Machine"

CLOSING MUSIC: Your favorite.

ANNOUNCEMENTS: Remind everyone to enjoy their memories of airplanes and to let them soar.

"ADULT DAY CARE ADDS TO CONTINUAL INDEPENDENCE, CAREGIVERS BENEFIT, STIMULATES EVEN ALZHEIMER'S VICTIMS, RELIEVES DEPRESSION AND ALSO ISOLATION."
— *Hugh Downs*

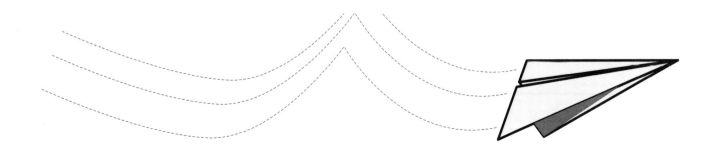

FLYING HIGH

ADAPTATIONS FOR TWO-YEAR-OLDS

Preparation: paper airplanes and music to "Hot Cross Buns"

Musical Warm Up: substitute "Zoom Song." for "Flying Song." To the tune of "Hot Cross Buns," sing one word: "Zoom, zoom, zoom." Talk about airplanes and rocket ships.

Interactive Song and/or Activities:

1. Kids' planes can zoom around the room while singing.
2. Everyone can enjoy aiming their airplanes at the balloons.

Repeat many times, then keep as a souvenir.

March/Movement: With plane in hand, march to the music—allowing plane to glide up and down many times. Land all planes on a grandfriends' lap.

RESOURCES:

All American Song Book
 "Daring Young Man (on the Flying Trapeze)" "Zoom Song." p. 140
Children's Songbook
 "Hot Cross Buns" p. 224
 "Old MacDonald Had a Farm" p. 96
Family songbook
 "I'm Forever Blowing Bubbles" p. 32
Greatest American Songbook
 "Army Air Corps Song" p. 10
Merry Christmas Songbook
 "Rudolph The Red Nosed Reindeer" p. 85
 "Angels We Have Heard on High" p. 30
Real Little Best Fake Book Ever
 "Let's All Sing Like the Birdies Sing" p. 367
Ultimate Fake Book
 "You're a Grand Old Flag" p. 665
 "Come Josephine in My Flying Machine" p, 107

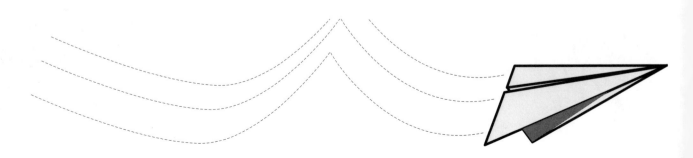

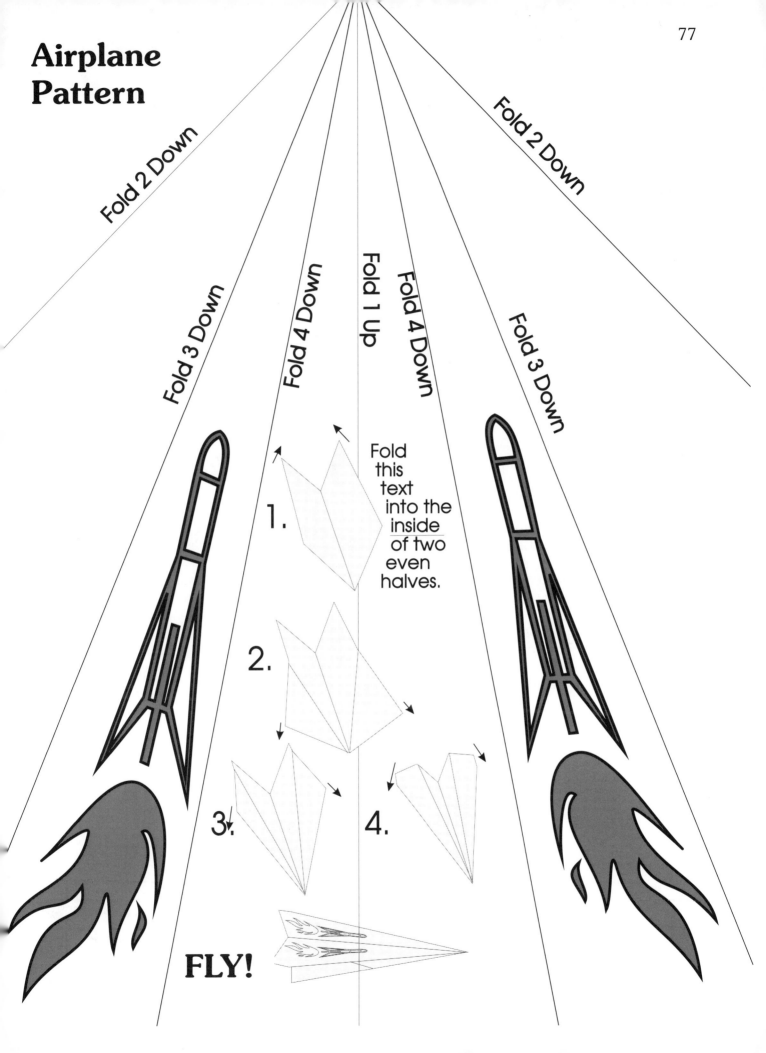

Program 13: HALLOWEEN

PREPARATION: Items needed inclued a large pumpkin, enough small pumpkins for each child, apron or smock, 2 knives, garbage pail, wet towel, heavy black magic markers, clothing and straw for pumpkin scarecrow, colored or printed (less scary than white) old sheets cut into ghost costumes with big eye holes for one child and one adult, fake microphone, hats (soldier, policeman, fireman, hard hat, chef, sports hats, cowboy, nurse, beekeeper, etc.) and a camera. Decorate hats with paint brushes, jewelry, flowers, money, candy, etc. Lighted jack-o-lantern is optional.

MUSIC: "The More We Get Together," "For He's a Jolly Good Fellow," "He's Got the Whole World in His Hands," "When the Saints Come Marching In," and "Skip to My Lou."

GREET SENIORS: One on one before the children enter.

RELAXING REHEARSAL: To the tune of "The More We Get Together," try this Halloween costume song and leave it open ended for imagination. "I'd like to be a _____, a _____, a _____, (teenager, power ranger, newscaster, sportswriter,) sung 3 times. End with "then I could _____."

Praise the jack-o-lantern in song—use the tune of "For He's a Jolly Good Fellow." Change the words to "He's a jolly good jack-o-lantern which nobody can deny."

OPENING SONG: Your favorite.

MUSICAL WARM UP: Introduce Halloween by announcing that a ghost will soon appear in the room to greet everyone. The child and adult in the ghost costumes should be hidden somewhere. Everyone sings the following words to the tune of "He's Got the Whole World in His Hands."

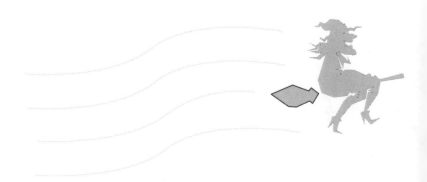

BOO To You

Here comes a fun-ny ghost— in-to our room.— Here comes a fun-ny ghost— in-to our room.— Here comes a fun-ny ghost— in-to our room.— Boo-oo-oo-oo— Boo!

2nd verse: Child floats around chairs, between people while all sing it again.
3rd verse: Ask everyone to sing louder and encourage another ghost.
4th verse: Adult in similar costume comes and floats around everywhere.

Adult ghost takes off his costume to reveal his identity and asks for everyone's input on their ideal Halloween costume. Use the fake or real microphone to obtain answers. Teach the children the Costume song that the adults rehearsed earlier. "I'd like to be a _____, a _____, a _____, then I would _____."

INTERACTIVE SONGS AND/OR ACTIVITIES: Make jack-o-lantern or scarecrows for each facility. Two people get to carve a pumpkin, a child with an assistant and an adult in front of the group. Wear aprons or smocks. A pumpkin becomes a jack-o-lantern when it is carved and a light is placed inside. No progress is evident until the group sings each section of the adapted song to the tune of "Skip to My Lou."

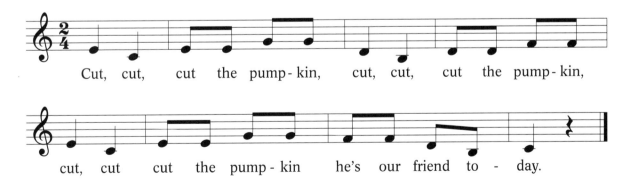

Cut, cut, cut the pump-kin, cut, cut, cut the pump-kin, cut, cut cut the pump-kin he's our friend to-day.

2nd verse: Clean the pumpkin—he's our friend today
3rd verse: Carve the pumpkin—he's our friend today
4th verse: Clothe the pumpkin—he's our friend today.

Dress pumpkin in any old clothes, add straw and present to each facility to display. Add a sign that indicates the intergenerational program.

Baby jack-o-lanterns: Adult ghost distributes black magic markers to several adults. Each child selects a small pumpkin, and a grandfriend to help them draw a face on it. While this intergenerational activity takes place, softly play "Skip to My Lou" as background music. Add the creators' initials on the backside. When faces are all drawn everyone sings together "For He's a Jolly Good Jack-O-Lantern, which nobody can deny." Children get to take their jack-o-lanterns home.

MARCH/MOVEMENT: Use your collection of hats for all. Children can carry their jack-o-lanterns and march to the music of "When the Saints go Marching In." Alter the words to "When the Hats Come Marching In." Decorated hats can be kept.

COOL DOWN: Talk about the hats and costumes seen today. Interview the kids on what costumes they do plan to wear for Halloween.

CLOSING MUSIC: Your usual favorite closing song.

ANNOUNCEMENTS: Halloween doesn't have to be scary. See if you can make someone happy this year with a smiling jack-o-lantern face of your own.

COOL DOWN: Name that tune that has a Halloween costume in the song title: "Santa Claus Is Coming to Town," "Here Comes Peter Cottontail," "Rock-a-Bye Baby," "Who's Afraid of the Big Bad Wolf?" "We're Off to See the Wizard" or "Baby Beluga."

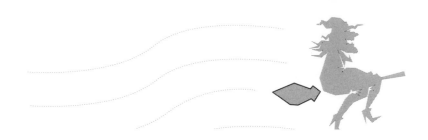

BOO To You

ADAPTATIONS FOR TWO-YEAR-OLDS

Interactive Activity: Only the adult carves the pumpkin so the children can see the process. Children can help scoop it out and plan the facial features. Magic markers can be used on the face instead of carving.

RESOURCES:

Legit Fake Book
- "For He's a Jolly Good Fellow" p. 107
- "He's Got the Whole World in His Hands" p. 133
- "When the Saints Go Marching In" p. 367

Wee Sing and Play
- "Skip to My Lou" p. 31
- "The More We Get Together"

Optional cool down songs are found in *Childrens Songbook* and *Raffi Children's Favorites*.

For additional ideas see *The Joy of Music in Maturity*
- "Healthy Fun" p. 395—389
- "Healthy Halloween" p. 391—395

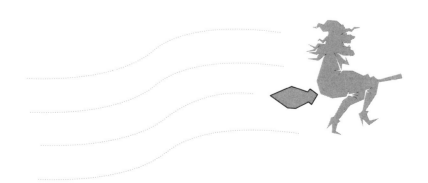

Program 14: HANDS ARE HANDY

PREPARATION: Children should previously trace their open hands on white paper and color or trace them onto colored construction paper. Be sure the child's name is on each tracing. Glue results on a tongue depressor. Items needed include a large inflatable globe or beach ball, a hand extender device from the OT dept., and a stuffed doll.

MUSIC: "If You're Happy and You Know it," "For He's a Jolly Good Fellow," "He's Got the Whole World in His Hands," and "Frere Jacques."

GREET SENIORS: One on one before children enter.

RELAXING REHEARSAL: Explain that today's theme is HANDS. Think of the many things they can do for which one can be grateful. Teach the song "Count Your Fingers" to the tune of "Frere Jacques." (See musical warm up.) Remind grandfriends that they are educating and affirming beginning arithmetic (now called math) for the children

OPENING SONG: Use the same song each session. Children bring paper hands to wave in the air. Collect all paper hands.

MUSICAL WARM UP: Sing "If You're Happy and You Know It" using action verses like:
   CLAP your hands
   SHAKE a hand
   Give a HUG

Sing "My Fingers are Starting to Wiggle" to the tune of "For He's a Jolly Good Fellow"
   My fingers are starting to wiggle—sung 3 times
   Wiggle and wiggle away.

Other verses with actions: toes (unseen), nose, and hands.

  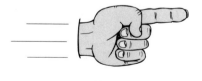

Hands are Handy

Sing "Count Your Fingers" ("Frere Jacques")

> Count your fingers, count your fingers
> On each hand, on each hand.
> 1-2-3-4-5, 1-2-3-4-5 (or to 10)
> On each hand, on each hand. (or both hands)

INTERACTIVE SONGS AND/OR ACTIVITIES:

- Sing "Count Your Fingers" while children count on their own hands as all sing. Children find a grandfriend to compare hand size and sing together as grandfriends help the children count fingers.

- Sing "He's Got the Whole World in His Hands." Both groups push the inflated world back and forth to one another.

- Discuss what hands can do: build, clap, touch, point, wave, share.

- Discuss that some hands don't work perfectly yet they still wave a greeting or are adaptable.

- Demonstrate a hand extender device. Let the children use it on some stuffed dolls.

"We've got the whole world in our hands"

MARCH/MOVEMENT: Pass out paper hands to children. March to the music while singing "If You're Happy and You Know It, give me Five." Children march and give grandfriends "five" with paper hands they have prepared earlier. Later the children can put down the paper hands and give an actual "high five" touch. Take some photos. Let children decide whether to keep their paper hand or give it to someone.

COOL DOWN: All seated while taking a good long look at their own hands. Show appreciation them by saying together: "Thank you hands." Blow a kiss with them or wave goodbye.

CLOSING MUSIC: Use the same song each session.

  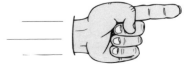

Hands are Handy

ANNOUNCEMENTS: Remember to thank your hands for all they have done in the past and all that they are going to do for you.

OPTIONAL ACTIVITY:

Touching activity: Use paper bags with items inside to touch without looking and guess their contents. Examples: popcorn, sponge, fur, comb, toothbrush.

Wall hanging: Have the adults and children trace their hands on colorful construction paper earlier in the week and display as a large poster with their names. Label it "Helping Hands." Transfer outline of hands to felt or fabric for a more permanent display or quilt top.

> **ADAPTATIONS FOR TWO-YEAR-OLDS**
>
> **Interactive Activity:** Show the different signs of friendship that each generation uses
> - Grandfriends give the children a handshake.
> - Children give the grandfriends a "high five" (upward palms together.)

"What's a high five?"

— Bertha, age 92

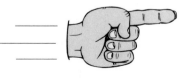

Hands are Handy

RESOURCES:

Children's Songbook
  "Frere Jacques" p. 234
Family Songbook of Faith and Joy
  "He's Got the Whole World
    in His Hands" p. 226
The Joy of Music in Maturity
  "If You're Happy and You Know It" p. 322
  Healthy Hands program pp. 367-372
Ultimate Fake Book
  "For He's a Jolly Good Fellow" p. 175

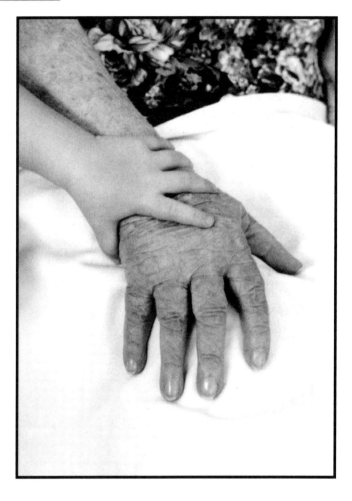

"A SOCIETY THAT CUTS OFF OLDER PEOPLE FROM MEANINGFUL CONTACT WITH CHILDREN...... IS GREATLY ENDANGERED. IN THE PRESENCE OF GRANDPARENT AND GRANDCHILD, PAST AND FUTURE MERGE IN THE PRESENT."
— *Margaret Mead*

Helpful Jobs

Program 15: JOBS

PREPARATION: Items needed include a bag filled with symbols of work such as garden tools, paint brushes, a computer keyboard, rolling pin, clothes pins, etc. Also a collection of hats such as cowboy, fireman, sailor, gardeners, baseball cap, nurses, or military hats. Large bag for each collection. Several small hand mirrors or small ones off the wall. Camera.

MUSIC: "Whistle While You Work," "If You're Happy and You Know It" (music handout) and "Here We Go Round the Mulberry Bush."

GREET SENIORS: One on one before children enter.

RELAXING REHEARSAL: Practice "Whistle While You Work" with attempts at whistling or singing la, la, la to the melody.

OPENING SONG: Your favorite.

MUSICAL WARM UP: Sing "Here We Go Round the Mulberry Bush" with these verses and using appropriate actions:
- This is the way we wash our clothes…(Note differences in the generations.)
- This is the way we iron our clothes…
- This is the way we mow the lawn…
- This is the way we wash the windows…
- This is the way we wash ourselves…(It's hard work getting your back clean.)

INTERACTIVE SONGS AND/OR ACTIVITIES:
- From a large bag have the children take turns pulling out objects that represent different forms of work. See suggestions in the above preparation section. Discuss. Note how times have changed in many instances. If the children are unaware of an object, have them ask a grandfriend and then report back to the group.

- Children pass out numerous hats for anyone to try on. Talk about the career or job involved. Let the grandfriends have some mirrors so the children can go up to them and see themselves.

Helpful Jobs

MARCH/MOVEMENT: Wearing a hat of their choice, children march to the music of "Whistle While You Work." Seniors should whistle or sing along. Take some pictures of this event. Collect all hats in two large bags

COOL DOWN: Adapt the tune of "If You're Happy and You Know It" to
1. If you worked and you know it clap your hands.
2. If you labored and you know it, give a groan.
3. If you're thankful (for the opportunity of working) say thank you.

Discuss each verse before singing giving praise for all forms of work and useful energy. Ask the children how they help out at home.

CLOSING MUSIC: Your favorite.

ANNOUNCEMENTS: Suggest that everyone do at least one helpful job today and that they whistle while they work.

> **ADAPTATIONS FOR TWO-YEAR-OLDS**
>
> **Musical Warm Up:** Talk about how helpful children can be when they are independently doing the following: Use the music to "The Mulberry Bush."
> 1. This is the way we wash our face
> 2. This is the way we brush our teeth
> 3. This is the way we get out of bed
> 4. This is the way we chase the dog (out of the house)
>
> **Interactive Songs and/or Activities:** Do only the hats that represent careers. Spend more time on those with potential action and sounds such as the fireman or policeman. Children should take them to a grandfriend and have them try it on. Use mirrors for all to enjoy the sight as well as the interaction.
>
> **Cool Down:** Children are seated. Sing "If You're Happy and You Know It Clap Your Hands" with the thought that you are happy to be able to be helpful with daily details such as brushing teeth etc.

Helpful Jobs

> **ADAPTATIONS FOR TWO-YEAR-OLDS (continued)**
>
> Additional verses might be:
>
> 1. If you wash your face daily let's do this—demonstrate
> 2. If you brush your teeth daily go like this
> 3. If you exercise daily give a stretch—Give thanks for one's working body even if some parts don't work well and *slowly* sing
> 4. If you're thankful for your body say "thank you."

RESOURCES:

Children's Songbook
   "Mulberry Bush" p. 216
   "If You're Happy and You Know It" p. 176
   "Whistle While You Work" p. 62

For additional ideas see *The Joy of Music in Maturity*
   "Labor of Love" p. 320-324

"Their mothers work away from home? Oh, my!"
— Milred, age 79

Hat's a Winner!

INTERGENERATIONAL SONG SHEET

If You're Happy And You Know It

Traditional

I Love You

Program 16: LOVE

PREPARATION: Items needed include paper plates with hearts, cupids or valentines pasted on them (pattern included), rhythm instruments.

MUSIC: "It's Love That Makes the World Go Round," (music handout) "I Love You Truly," "I Love You" (from the Barney show), "The Happy Wanderer," and "Goodnight Ladies."

GREET SENIORS: One on one before children enter.

RELAXING REHEARSAL: Teach the song "It's Love That Makes the World Go Round." Review music for "I Love You Truly."

OPENING SONG: Your favorite.

MUSICAL WARM UP: Teach everyone "It's Love That Makes the World Go Round." Start with adults singing. Children join in as it becomes familiar.

1st verse:	"It's Love, It's Love, It's Love That Makes the World Go Round."
2nd verse:	It's you, It's you, It's you,… (Sung while pointing to kids.)
3rd verse:	It's me, It's me, It's me,… (Sung while pointing to self.)
4th verse:	It's us, It's us, It's us,… (Sung with raised arms.)

I love you, too.

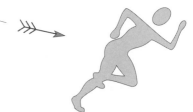

I LOVE YOU

Kids can sing "I Love You" — Barney version

> I love you, you love me.
> We're a happy family.
> With a great big hug
> And a kiss from me to you,
> Won't you say you love me too?
>
> I love you, you love me,
> We're best friends like friends should be,
> With a great big hug
> And a kiss from me to you,
> Won't you say you love me too?

"I Love You" Lyrics by Lee Bernstein
©1983 Shimbarah Music, a division of the Lyons Group. Used with permission

> "GENERATION CAN MEAN AGE GROUP, BIRTH COHORT OR LINEAGE WITHIN FAMILIES."
> — from *Ties That Bind*

During the singing everyone should give high fives to a grandfriend or hug oneself or hug another.

INTERACTIVE SONGS AND/OR ACTIVITIES: Use paper plates with hearts pasted on them. Have the children distribute them to their grandfriends. Exercise with music by following the leader to the following songs:

"I LOVE You Truly" — Use round circular motions. Adults can sing to the children while exercising with plates.
"I LOVE You" (Barney song) — Make fanning motions.
"The Happy Wanderer" (I LOVE to go a Wandering) — Tap knees, head, shoulders following leader's motions. Keep all of the rhythmic action in groups of eight.

MARCH/MOVEMENT: March to "The Happy Wanderer." Suggest that seniors LOVE their hands and clap them while kids march around following a leader. Children could choose a rhythm instrument they LOVE and march with it.

OPTIONAL ACTIVITY: At the microphone, kids and adults tell who they love. Include people or animals. Prompt with "I Love _____." Soft background music if appropriate.

CLOSING MUSIC: Use the same music to close every session.

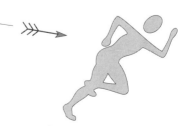

I LOVE YOU

ANNOUNCEMENTS: Enjoy being a loving person. Announce the next program including date, time, and Theme. Distribute copies of "It's Love that Makes the World Go Round" for review, bulletin boards or scrapbooks and to share with families and friends.

> **ADAPTATIONS FOR TWO-YEAR-OLDS**
>
> **Preparation:** Cut out felt (or paper) pink, red and white hearts. A basket is useful to hold hearts (or valentines.)
>
> **Musical Warm Up:** Teach the song "Who Can Find the Valentine?" to the tune of "O Du Lieber Augustin."
>
> Who can find the valentine, valentine, valentine,
> Who can find the valentine?
> My valentine's _____ (give the color).
>
> Teacher holds up the color of a valentine while children name their color. All sing through several colors
>
> **Interactive Song and/or Activities:**
> - Leader instructs children to pass out valentines by color to their grandfriends.
> - Repeat the Valentine song as each color gets recognized.
> - Remind the adults that they are helping with the children's education today.
> - Leader calls out one color and the children collect that color. They place it in a pretty basket or they can tape the heart to each persons clothing. Do this song three times until all are collected.

RESOURCES:

The Joy of Music in Maturity
   "It's Love that Makes the World Go Round" p. 70
Raffi Children's Favorites
   "This Old Man" p. 156
Ultimate Fake Book
   "Happy Wanderer" p. 204
   "I Love You Truly" p. 238

Wee Sing Children's Songs
   "Good Night" p. 50
1001 Jumbo Words and Music
   "Ach! Du Lieber Augustin" p. 354

For additional ideas see
The Joy of Music in Maturity
   "I Love You and Me" p. 68-72
   "It's Valentine Love" p 73-79

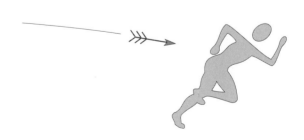

Some Valentine Hearts

INTERGENERATIONAL SONG SHEET

It's Love That Makes the World Go 'Round

Words and music: Traditional

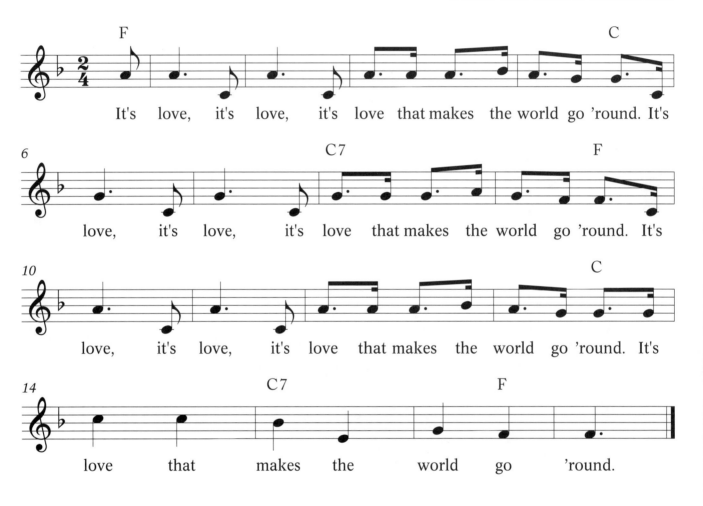

It's love, it's love, it's love that makes the world go 'round. It's love, it's love, it's love that makes the world go 'round. It's love, it's love, it's love that makes the world go 'round. It's love that makes the world go 'round.

INTERGENERATIONAL SONG SHEET

Who Can Find the Valentine?

(to the melody of "O Du lieber Augustin")

Words: J. Shaw   Music: German Folksong

Who can find the Val-en-tine, Val-en-tine, Val-en-tine?

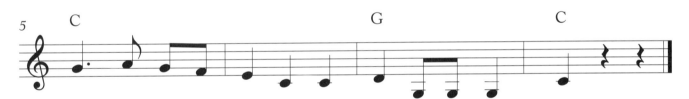

Who can find the Val-en-tine? My Val-en-tine's (Color)

School Bells

Program 17: SCHOOL

PREPARATION: Items needed include a school bell, large American flag, and school props. (Lunch box, brown paper lunch bag, apple, chalk, erasers, blackboard, dunce cap, ruler, and calculator.)

MUSIC: "If You're Happy and You Know It," "Ten Little Indians," "Did You Ever See a Lassie?," "Bingo," "School Days," "Do-Re-Mi," "Alphabet Song," and "You're a Grand Old Flag."

GREET SENIORS: One on one before children enter.

RELAXING REHEARSAL: Grandfriends should review the old song "School Days" to sing to the children later in the program. Also review the Pledge of Allegiance.

> I pledge allegiance to the flag
> of the United States of America
> and to the Republic for which it stands,
> One nation, under God, indivisible,
> with liberty and justice for all.

OPENING SONG: Use the same song each session.

MUSICAL WARM UP: Leader rings the school bell to command everyone's attention and to welcome them to today's program called "School Bells." Recall the use of the school bell to beckon pupils to school. Grandfriends sing the 1907 song "School Days" to the children.

> School days, school days,
> dear old golden rule days.
> Readin' and 'ritin' and 'rithmetic,
> taught to the tune of a hickr'y stick,
> You were my queen in calico,
> I was your bashful barefoot beau,
> and you wrote on my slate, I love you Joe,
> When we were a couple of kids.

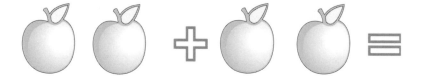

School Bells

Use your slate or blackboard and write the letters M-O-M-M-Y in large print. Explain that everyone is going to sing about someone who loves them and have a spelling lesson at the same time. Use the spelling song to the tune of "Bingo." Adapt the song to any five-letter word. Mention that this will be a special exercise in preparation for the actual school program coming up. For example:

Someone loves me very much
and Mommy is her name, oh
M-O-M-M-Y, M-O-M-M-Y, M-O-M-M-Y
and mommy is her name, oh.

Additional verses could include daddy, or anyone's five-letter name—even "grama" with an explanation that this spelling is just for fun. Address the fact that even if someone's mommy is deceased they are still loved by them.

You might want to pretend to put on your thinking cap with the motions of placing a cap on your head and tying it under your chin. Sing the following song in preparation for class to the tune of "If You're Happy and You Know It."

If you're thinking and you know it, clap your hands
If you're thinking and you know it, clap your hands,
If you're thinking and you know it, then your face will surely show it,
If you're thinking and you know it, clap your hands.

Verse 2: If you're smart and you know it… (assure everyone on this)
Verse 3: If you're alert and you know it…

Declare that everyone is now ready for school.

INTERACTIVE SONGS AND/OR ACTIVITIES: Ring the school bell and welcome the chlidren to their day school. Give it an appropriate name. Ring the bell for each new activity.

Pledge: Open with the Pledge of Allegiance led by the grandfriends. Have every one stand if possible. Children and grandfriends should share in holding the flag up together. Practice the words first before pledging. Announce that everyone should be seated and that school is now in session.

Arithmetic/Math: Have everyone hold up their hand and slowly sing to the tune of "Ten Little Indians" these adapted words:

One little, two little, three little fingers,
Four little, five little six little fingers,
Seven little, eight little, nine little fingers
Ten little fingers on my hand

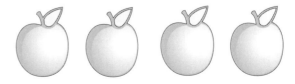

School Bells

Invite the children to go to their grandfriends and count their fingers. Change the words of the song to "One large, two large, three big fingers." Children should put their palm on a grandfriends palm and compare sizes. Take photos. If time permits reverse the order of the song to "Ten little, nine little, eight little fingers." Ring the bell for

History: Ask the children the following questions and give them permission to ask their grandfriends for the answer if they are unsure of it.

1. Who is the president of the United States?
2. What is his wife's name?
3. Where do they live?
4. Where do most of our laws get formed?
5. How many states are there in the U.S. or how many stars on the flag?

Ring the school bell to announce that the next class is...

Education: In your prepared large box or bag, have the children pull out a school item. Ask them to guess what it is. All sing to the tune of "Did You Ever See a Lassie?"

Did you ever take a lunch box, a lunch box, a lunch box,
did you ever take a lunch box like this to your school?—Discuss.
What was in your lunch box, your lunch box, your lunch box,
Oh what was in your lunch box that you took to school? —Discuss

Other verses to be sung and compared:
Did you ever wear a dunce cap at...
Did you ever clap erasers... (clap erasers, watch chalk dust)
Did you ever take an apple to the teacher...
Did you ever take a ruler....Discuss calculators used today.

Ring the bell many times to announce that school is over. Praise them for excellent work.

MARCH/MOVEMENT: Using rhythm band instruments to represent music class, march using the following songs:

"Do-Re-Mi"
"Alphabet Song"
"You're a Grand Old Flag "

COOL DOWN: Everyone should be seated. Praise everyone for being so smart during the classroom session. Remind them that learning is forever. Talk about all the things you don't learn in school that you learn at home, church, supermarket or walking outdoors.

School Bells

CLOSING MUSIC: Use the same song each session

ANNOUNCEMENTS: Ask everyone to learn something new after they leave the program today and talk about it with each other.

> **ADAPTATIONS FOR TWO-YEAR-OLDS**
>
> **Preparation:** Determine how many grandfriends have previously taught school and have enough fresh red apples for presentation
>
> Shorten the program by eliminating some of the sections of your choice. Also have the children present each grandfriend who once taught school a fresh apple. Sing the song "If You're Smart and You Know It, Clap Your Hands" and present everyone with some apple slices as a treat. Talk about the origin of an apple for the teacher.

RESOURCES:

Children's Songbook
 "Alphabet Song" p. 212
 "Bingo" p. 124
 "Do-Re-Mi" p 44
 "If You're Happy and You Know It" p. 176
 "Ten Little Indians" p. 217
Ultimate Fake Book
 "School Days" p. 481
 "You're a Grand Old Flag" p. 665
Wee Sing and Play
 "Did You Ever See a Lassie?" p. 28

For additional ideas see *The Joy of Music in Maturity*
 "Dear Old School Days" p. 325-332

"THE 'ELDER FUNCTION' REFERS TO THE NATURAL PROPENSITY OF THE OLD TO SHARE WITH THE YOUNG THE ACCUMULATED KNOWLEDGE AND EXPERIENCE THEY HAVE COLLECTED."
— Dr. Robert Butler

SMILES are SUPER

Program 18: SMILES

PREPARATION: Items needed include empty picture frames, yellow plastic plates with simple black smiles marked on each, and the individual yellow cardboard letters of S-M-I-L-E. The "Smiles" music handouts are for all to keep.

MUSIC: "Smiles," (music handout) "Alphabet Song," "Bingo" and "London Bridge."

GREET SENIORS: One on one before children enter.

RELAXING REHEARSAL: Grandfriends renew the old song "Smiles" with a rehearsal. The goal is to introduce this "golden oldie" to the children later in the program.

OPENING SONG: Use the same song each session.

MUSICAL WARM UP: All sing the entire "Alphabet Song" (A-B-C-D) as a warm-up. Then have everyone sing it only to the first letter of the word smile. When they reach letter "S" have a child hold up that letter for all to see. Proceed until the entire word is sung with each child holding up his letter as it is called in front of the group. Arrange a group picture when all five are smiling and standing in correct order.

INTERACTIVE SONGS AND/OR ACTIVITIES: Ask another five children to participate and share the letters with their grandfriends. Sing the song holding up the appropriate letters. Photograph another group of five. Discuss what makes you smile. The following are suggested as open questions:
1. If I make a funny face will you smile?
2. What happens when you see a baby?
3. What animal makes you smile?
4. Do you smile when you see your grandparents or grandchildren?
5. What does make you smile?

Practice making your prettiest smile with the empty frames. Let the children take the frame to a grandfriend and frame their face. Try child and adult in the same picture. More smiles. More photos.

SMILES are SUPER

MARCH/MOVEMENT: Pass out the yellow smile plates two for each child, one for each adult. Instruct the children to march clapping two smile plates together. The seated adults should clap the plate on their leg to the rhythm of the music. March to "Smiles."

COOL DOWN: Grandfriends should sing the song "Smiles" a 1917 song by Callahan and Roberts. Words are provided on a song sheet to take home.

CLOSING MUSIC: Use the same song each session.

ANNOUNCMENTS: Remind everyone that a smile is a gift when you give it away, that it is fun to do and costs nothing. Encourage people to smile more often and watch for results. Everyone should take home their music handouts of the words as a souvenir of the song and its lasting value.

OPTIONAL ACTIVITY: Recommend that all who plan to attend wear something yellow. Announce well in advance with posters, intercommunication, or a notice. Photograph and display all the sunshine and smiles of this program.

Smile contest: The children can move around the room and choose the person with the largest smile. Winner gets their picture taken which eventually gets posted.

Smile cheer: Using the letters of S-M-I-L-E, leader yells "Give me an 'S'" and someone holds up that letter. Continue until the word is spelled. End with "What does that spell?" "What makes me happy?"

ADAPATATIONS FOR TWO-YEAR-OLDS

Preparation: Items needed include a collection of hand held mirrors, music to "Old MacDonald Had a Farm."

Musical Warm Up: Sing the following lyrics to the tune of "Old MacDonald Had a Farm," using the child's name where indicated.

> _____(name) had a smile, S-M-I-L-E
> and on her face she had a smile S-M-I-L-E
> With a smile right here and a smile right there
> Here a smile, there a smile, everywhere a smile, smile
> _____ had a smile, S-M-I-L-E.

Choose an adult, use their name and have the children watch that big smile.

ADAPATATIONS FOR TWO-YEAR-OLDS (continued)

Interactive Songs and/or Activities: Pass out hand held mirrors to the children and do the above song and activity. Ask them to find a grandfriend to look in the mirror and sing along. Children should collect the mirrors. Next have them pass out the yellow smile plates to everyone attending. Have the adults hold them up in front of their own faces for the children to enjoy. Then have the children hold the plate in front of their face for their grandfriends.

Sing the following to the tune of "London Bridge" with appropriate facial expressions:

No one has a frown like mine, frown like mine, frown like mine.
No one has a frown like mine, I am saaaaaaaaaad.
No one has a smile like mine, smile like mine, smile like mine.
No one has a smile like mine, I am happy.
No one has a laugh like mine, laugh like mine, laugh like mine,
No one has a laugh like mine, I am silly.

RESOURCES:

Children's Songbook
  "Alphabet Song" p. 212
  "Bingo" p. 124
  "London Bridge" p. 230
Family Songbook
  "Smiles" p. 34

For additional ideas see
The Joy of Music in Maturity
  "Everyone Loves a Smile"
  p. 93-97

"Their faces are wrinkled from smiling so much."

— Jason, age 4

INTERGENERATIONAL SONG SHEET

Smiles
(1917)

Words: J. Will Callahan

Music: Lee S. Roberts

Outer Space is the Place!

Program 19: OUTER SPACE

PREPARATION: Items needed include Martian headbands (pattern included), helium balloons (each tied with a six foot string and attached to chairs and wheelchairs), one balloon with paper feet attached and face drawn on it to represent a space man, and a large parachute. Suggest that all may dress in a silly fashion by wearing their clothing inside out or backwards. Optional items from families that are space related like rockets, robots, and moon boots, and head antennae can also be used.

MUSIC: "Ring Around the Rosy," "Twinkle, Twinkle, Little Star," "Hey Diddle, Diddle," and taped music from *Star Wars*, "Stardust," or "Would You Like to Swing on a Star" and "When You Wish Upon a Star."

GREET SENIORS: One on one before the children enter.

RELAXING REHEARSAL: Prepare for a space trip by teaching the following adapted words to "Ring Around the Rosie."

> Ring around the rocket ship
> Fly up to the stars
> Outer space, outer space
> Fall where you are.
>
> 5-4-3-2-1 blast off. (spoken)

Practice pulling down the balloons, singing this song, and releasing the balloon on the words "Blast off."

OPENING SONG: Use your favorite song for every session.

MUSICAL WARM UP: Sing songs together about space/sky.

"Twinkle, Twinkle Little *Star*"— use actions
"You are My *Sunshine*" with actions
"Hey Diddle, Diddle" (cow jumped over the *moon*)

Outer Space is the Place!

INTERACTIVE SONGS AND/OR ACTIVITIES: Let the children put on the Martian head bands. The grandfriends can help adjust the size.

- Moon walk—Ask everyone to use very large slow movements to the music of "Star Dust" or a similar slow tempo song. Lift knees high, move arms up and down slowly. Children may hold hands with a grandfriend and move arms slowly together.

- When Neil Armstrong stepped onto the moon, he said, "That's one small step for man, one giant leap for mankind." Have the children take small steps and giant leaps pretending they are on the moon.

- Teach the children "Ring Around the Rocket Ship." Have them walk around in a circle, holding hands, for the first three lines. Crouch down when singing "Fall where you are" and then count "5-4-3-2-1 blast off" with the kids jumping high. The adults should sing with their balloons pulled down to chair height and release the balloon when they sing "blast off."

MARCH/MOVEMENT: Feature the "Martian Parade" using rhythm instruments including some that sound unusual. Use space music such as "Swinging on a Star."

COOL DOWN: When everyone is seated, play the music to "When You Wish Upon a Star" and see if anyone can identify it. Have everyone sing "Twinkle, Twinkle Little Star." Ask if anyone knows the rhyme "Star Light, Star Bright." (Today's ending to that is "Oh, gee it's a satellite.") Say it in unison. Ask if anyone would like to make a wish when they see the next star. What would they wish for?

CLOSING MUSIC: Use the same song each session.

ANNOUNCEMENTS: Think of all the wonders that space provides. Thank everyone for having a fun adventure in space. Give children a balloon as they leave. They may keep the Martian headbands or give it to a grandfriend.

OPTIONAL ACTIVITY: Use large parachute alternating adult and child in a large circle. Everyone should hold on to it. Move parachute up and down slowly to any "space music." Give the balloon spaceman a space walk.

"THE OUTSTANDING CHARACTERISTIC OF THE ELDERLY, NOW AND IN THE FUTURE, IS THEIR DIVERSITY. THERE IS NO SUCH THING AS A 'TYPICAL OLDER PERSON.'"
— from *Ties That Bind*

Outer Space is the Place!

ADAPTATIONS FOR TWO-YEAR-OLDS

Interactive Songs and/or Activities: If children are too young to form a circle for "Ring Around a Rocket Ship," then have them spin slowly individually. Continue as before with the kids falling to the floor and blasting off.

Repeat the song "Ring Around the Rocket Ship" and have each child find a grandfriend. Together they pull down the balloon, sing the song, and let it go together as they say "blast off." Eliminate the moon walk.

RESOURCES:

Children's Songbook
    "Mulberry Bush" p. 216
Disney Collection
    "When You Wish Upon a Star" p. 129
Festival of Popular Songs
    "You are My Sunshine" p. 230
Wee Sing Nursery Rhymes and Lullabies
    "Hey Diddle, Diddle" p. 40
    "Twinkle, Twinkle Little Star" p. 46

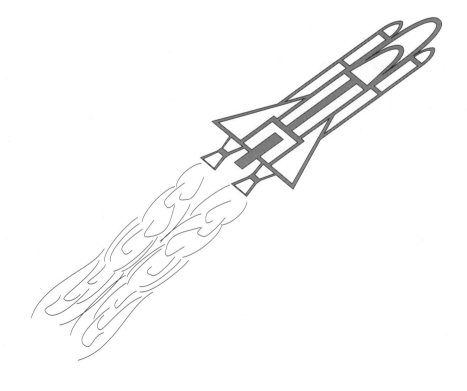

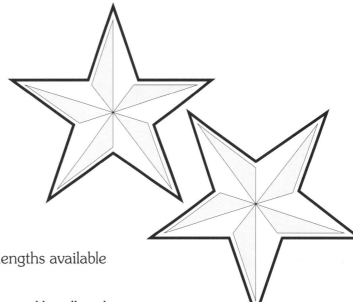

MARTIAN HEADBAND DIRECTIONS:

Materials: Pipe cleaners, preferably the long lengths available from craft stores, transparent tape, paper.

1. Copy this page and cut out the stars above and headband fronts below. (Lay the first cutouts over the page for copy 2 to double your output.)

2. If convenient, add color to the headbands and glitter to the stars.

3. Cut strips of paper to complete the headbands to a length of about 22" and tape onto headband fronts.

4. Attach pipe cleaners to the inside front of the headband with both ends sticking up in the air about 4" and attach stars to those ends with tape.

5. Fit headbands to children using tape to close the circle.

Program 20: SPRING

PREPARATION: Items needed include umbrellas—especially child-sized, large bean or flower seeds, potting soil in flower pots or paper cups, small watering pitcher (filled) and a damp towel. Hide large seeds under the adult chairs before the children arrive. A tape with prerecorded sounds of spring is desirable. This can be good project for scouts or volunteers.

MUSIC: "April Showers," "The Ants Go Marching," "Found a Peanut," "Hokey-Pokey," "Stars and Stripes Forever."

GREET SENIORS: One on one before the children enter.

RELAXING REHEARSAL: Rehearse the song "April Showers."

OPENING SONG: your favorite

MUSICAL WARM UP: All sing "The Ants Go Marching " to the old tune of "When Johnny Comes Marching Home" since it's about ants getting out of the rain.

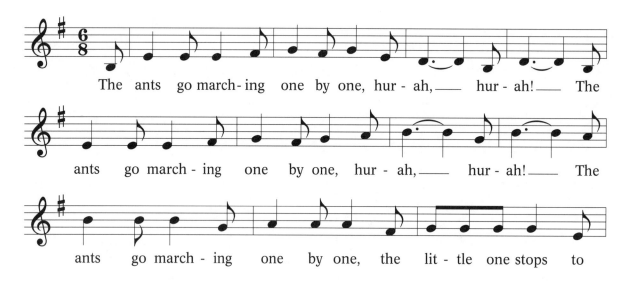

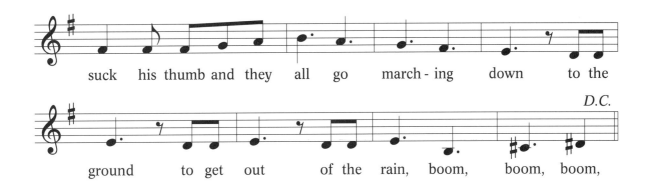

suck his thumb and they all go march-ing down to the ground to get out of the rain, boom, boom, boom, *D.C.*

2. Ants go marching two by two—and the little one stops to tie his shoe…
3. Three by three—and the little one stops cause he skins his knee…
4. Four by four—and the little one stops to shut the door…
5. Five by five—and the little one says I'm glad we're alive…

Administrator or other designated person can shout or lead the hurrah parts. A drum can be used to augment the boom boom section.

INTERACTIVE SONGS AND/OR ACTIVITIES:

Spring Fling: Many people feel like dancing when spring arrives. This is the Intergenerational Spring Fling. Do the "Hokey-Pokey"—only change the words to "Springy Flingy."

You put your left hand in, you take your left hand out,
You put your left hand in, and you shake it all about.
You do the spring flingy (hands shaking above head)
   and you run to your grandfriend, (run up to anyone)
That's what it's all about.

Verse 2: You put your right hand in…take the grandfriends hand and together put in your right hand.
Verse 3: You put your left foot in…with children in front of their grandfriends.
Verse 4: You put your right foot in…
Verse 5: You put your head in…
Verse 6: You put whole self in…children return to center circle and all sing.

SPRING FLING

Planting Time: Children hunt under chairs for garden seeds and sing the song written below. Then they pass out flower pots that have been filled with potting soil and ask their grandfriends to hold them. All sing verse two. Sing verse three while children stick their finger in the soil and plant their seeds. Finally sing verse four for watering. Use the adapted words to "Found a Peanut" as follows:

Found a garden seed, found a garden seed,
found a garden seed just now.
Just now I found a garden seed,
found a garden seed just now.

Verse 2: Shared a flower pot...
Verse 3: Put the seed in...
Verse 4: I need water...

An adult with a small watering can should carefully water each one. Plants can be taken home or left in an indoor garden area to be observed at subsequent sessions. As plants mature, they can be transplanted outdoors. A damp towel may be necessary for clean up.

MARCH/MOVEMENT: Open with the chant: "Rain rain, go away, come again another day, little _____(name) wants to play." Repeat for as many names as possible. Then open up an umbrella indoors in spite of the gasps that this means bad luck. Explain about superstition and celebrate spring with an indoor umbrella march. Each child can march with their umbrella, adults can open up theirs if they wish to add to the decor and camaraderie. March to the music of "April Showers" and ask the grandfriends to sing along. Conclude with the "Stars and Stripes Forever" sometimes known as "Be Kind to Your Web-Footed Friends." When the march is over, close all of the umbrellas and have everyone sit down.

COOL DOWN: Listen to any sounds of spring. They can be pre-recorded. Examples: Happy children in a play yard, bullfrogs, peepers, rain on the roof, baby chicks, birds, crack of a baseball bat or tricycles running.

CLOSING MUSIC: Use your favorite song for closure.

ANNOUNCEMENTS: Watch closely for things that are growing—including the size of the children or grandchildren.

OPTIONAL ACTIVITY: Ant headbands for the children and the leader. Use paper strips and black pipe cleaners which have curled ends (pattern included in Summer program, p.115.)

SPRING FLING

> **ADAPTATIONS FOR TWO-YEAR-OLDS**
> **Musical Warm Up:** Hold up fingers for each number of ants in the song. Replace any activity with these two favorite action songs:
> "Baby Bumblebee" (bees help the flowers)
> "Eentsy Weentsy Spider" (down came the rains)

RESOURCES:

Family Songbook of Faith and Joy
  "April Showers" p. 30
Legit Fake Book
  "Stars and Stripes Forever" p. 450
Wee Sing and Play Musical Games
  "The Hokey-Pokey" p. 19
Wee Sing Children's Songs
  "Eentsy Weentsy Spider " p. 8
Wee Sing Silly Songs
  "The Ants Go Marching" p. 40
  "Be Kind to Your Web Footed Friends" p. 43
  "Found a Peanut" p. 46
  "Baby Bumblebee" p. 37

For additional ideas see *The Joy of Music in Maturity*
  "Spring Has Sprung" p. 186-190
  "Spring March" p. 146-148
Refer to program in this book "Chinese New Year"

"THE CONTINUITY OF ALL CULTURE DEPENDS ON THE LIVING PRESENCE
OF AT LEAST THREE GENERATIONS."
— *Margaret Mead*

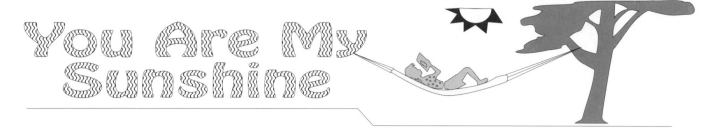

Program 21: SUMMER

PREPARATION: Items needed include ant headbands (pattern included) a sun hat, checkered picnic tablecloth, sunshine face frames (pattern included), mirrors, a camera, plus a picnic basket filled with summer items such as sunglasses, suntan lotion, small ball, bikini suit, fan, fly swatter, seashell, flower and garden seeds.

MUSIC: Food songs such as "Apples and Bananas," "Peanut Butter Sandwich," "Don't Sit Under the Apple Tree," "Hot Cross Buns," "Take Me Out To the Ball Game," "The Muffin Man," "Yes, We Have No Bananas," and "On Top of Spaghetti." Also "You Are My Sunshine," "Battle Hymn of the Republic" and "Here We Go Round the Mulberry Bush."

GREET SENIORS: One on one before the children enter.

RELAXING REHEARSAL: Sing "You are My Sunshine."

OPENING SONG: Your favorite song that you use for each session.

MUSICAL WARM UP: Summer activities sung to the tune of "Here We Go Round the Mulberry Bush."

This is the way we fan ourselves, fan ourselves, fan ourselves,
This is the way we fan ourselves on a summer morning.

Verse 2: Swim a lot (lots of strokes).
Verse 3: Eat ice cream (big licks).
Verse 4: Swat a fly (splat).
Verse 5: Itch all over.

INTERACTIVE SONGS AND/OR ACTIVITIES:
Picnic Identification: Place a picnic tablecloth on the floor and bring out your prepared picnic basket full of summer items to be guessed. A child should reach in the basket, feel the item and announce what it is. If he can't identify it, he should take it to a grandfriend and ask for the answer, then place it on the picnic tablecloth. Allow time for discussion. Ask the child to take the basket to a grandfriend and let them try this activity.

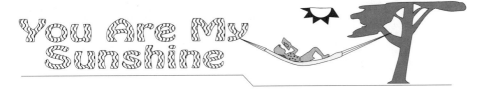

You Are My Sunshine

Sunshine Faces: You truly are my sunshine is the theme for the interaction of these generations. Leader should wear a sunshine face frame to introduce this section. Let the children distribute the prepared sun faces. Use mirrors to let everyone enjoy their sunshine faces. Group singing of "You Are My Sunshine." Point to each other when you repeat the song. Be sure to take a group photo of all who participate.

MARCH/MOVEMENT: Wearing these sunshine faces, children march around to the "Battle Hymn of the Republic." Collect the faces and allow everyone to keep them as a reminder of this sunny event.

COOL DOWN: Picnic foods in song: play the following songs or sing just the melody for song identification. All songs have a picnic food in the title or somewhere in the song.

Muffin Man
Don't Sit Under the *Apple* Tree
Hot Cross *Buns*
Take me Out to the Ball Game (*peanuts* and *cracker jack*)
Peanut Butter Sandwich
Apples and Bananas
Yes, We Have No *Bananas*
On Top of *Spaghetti*

CLOSING MUSIC: Your traditional closer.

ANNOUNCEMENTS: Think of other people who bring sunshine into your life. Tell them so the next time you see them.

OPTIONAL ACTIVITY: Summertime taste treat of ice cold lemonade or ice cream. Fans made from folded paper. (See Appendix D)

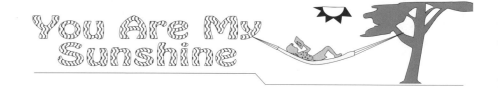

You Are My Sunshine

> **ADAPTATIONS FOR TWO-YEAR-OLDS**
>
> **Preparation:** Prepare a felt board with an outline of a child in a bathing suit and a blue piece of felt representing water. The water should be large enough to reach the child's waist. Leader sings the music. (Handout, p.115.)
>
> **Cool Down:** Substitute with this felt board activity. As the song is sung, respond with rhythmic clapping. Follow the words by having the felt cover the child's toes, ankles, knees, legs, and ending at the waist on the felt board.

RESOURCES:

Children's Songbook
  "Hot Cross Buns" p. 224
  "Mulberry Bush" p. 216
  "On Top of Spaghetti" p. 128
Festival of Popular Songs
  "You are My Sunshine" p. 230
Legit Fake Book
  "Battle Hymn of the Republic" p. 40
  "Don't Sit Under the Apple Tree" p. 89
Popular Songs That Live Forever
  "Take Me Out to the Ball Game" p. 222

Raffi Children's Favorites
  "Apples and Bananas" p. 14
  "Peanut Butter Sandwich" p. 140
Treasury of Best Loved Songs
  "Yes, We Have No Bananas" p. 202
Wee Sing and Play Musical Games
  "Muffin Man" p. 20

For additional ideas see *The Joy of Music in Maturity*
  "Porches Were Precious" p. 288-292
  "Ice Cream–It's Cool" p. 311-316
  "Take Me Out to the Ballgame" p. 239-244

"VERY LITTLE DATA EXISTS TO COMMENT ON THE VALUE OF BRINGING CHILDREN AND SENIORS TOGETHER. STILL SOME EXPERTS HAVE NOTICED A SPECIAL BOND BETWEEN CHILDREN AND ELDERS."
— *Hugh Downs*

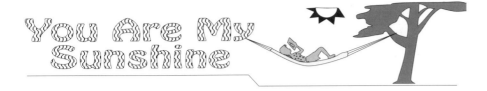

ANT HEADBAND DIRECTIONS

Materials: Pipe cleaners, preferably black, long lengths available from craft stores, transparent tape, paper.

1. Copy this page and cut out the headband fronts below. (Lay the first cutouts over the page for copy 2 to double your output.)

2. Cut strips of paper to complete the headbands to a length of about 22" and tape onto headband fronts.

3. Attach pipe cleaner to the inside front of the headband with both ends sticking up in the air about 5" and bend ends into circular loops.

4. Fit headbands to children using tape to close the circle.

SUNSHINE HAT PATTERN

DIRECTIONS:

1. Copy this page onto heavier paper for use as a pattern and cut along the lines.

2. Fold sheets of bright 9 x 12" construction paper in half to form 9 x 6" folders.

3. Lay the pattern on the folded sheet with the "Fold Line" superimposed and trace the pattern. Cut along the lines while the construction paper is still folded. The result will be a burst of sunshine.

4. Fold the square tabs below on the dotted lines and apply tape to hold them and add strength.

5. Punch a hole in each tab and feed the string or elastic through to hold onto child's head.

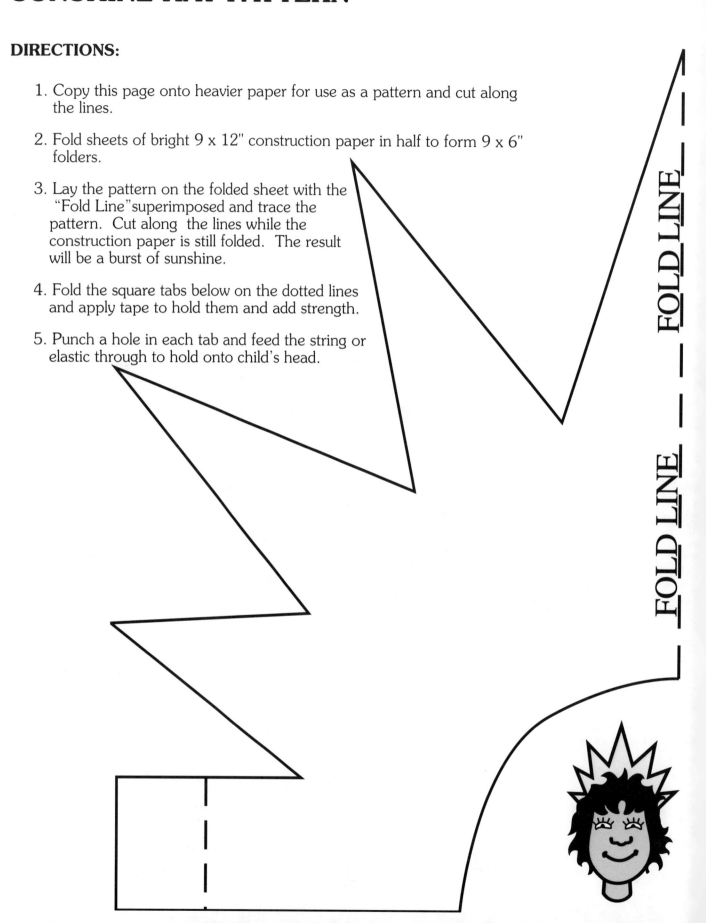

INTERGENERATIONAL SONG SHEET

Swim Song

Words and music: Joan Shaw

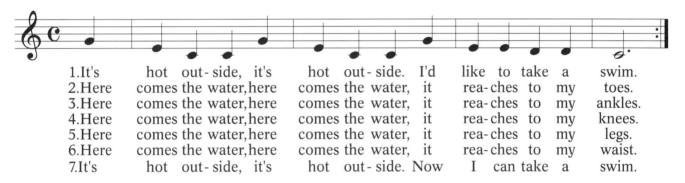

1. It's hot out-side, it's hot out-side. I'd like to take a swim.
2. Here comes the water, here comes the water, it rea-ches to my toes.
3. Here comes the water, here comes the water, it rea-ches to my ankles.
4. Here comes the water, here comes the water, it rea-ches to my knees.
5. Here comes the water, here comes the water, it rea-ches to my legs.
6. Here comes the water, here comes the water, it rea-ches to my waist.
7. It's hot out-side, it's hot out-side. Now I can take a swim.

Thankful Living

Program 22: THANKSGIVING

PREPARATION: Items needed include a pop-up tent, Indian headbands for children (pattern included), large posterboard on an easel with the letters T-H-A-N-K-F-U-L written clearly down the left edge, black marking pen, and "Bringing in the Sheaves" printed music handout (included.)

MUSIC: "Ten Little Indians," "Frere Jacques," "Turkey in the Straw" (music handout.)

GREET SENIORS: One on one before children enter.

RELAXING REHEARSAL: Review the old song "Bringing in the Sheaves." Use the handout.

OPENING SONG: Use the same song each session.

MUSICAL WARM UP: Pass out headbands to the children who are seated, so they can pretend to be Indians at the earliest Thanksgiving. Everyone should sing "Ten Little Indians" and have a child pop up with each number. Modernize the song to:

> One little two little, three little Indians,
> Four little, five little, six little Indians,
> Seven little, eight little, nine little Indians,
> Ten little Indian BOYS AND GIRLS.

Demonstrate the modern pop-up tent. Ask anyone familiar to assist. Sing the song again and have the children enter the tent until all ten are inside. Sing once more and have them pop out. Invite ten more people to enter the tent, any age. Discuss how the Indians gathered crops for the first Thanksgiving dinner to share with the Pilgrims who had landed in Massachusetts.

INTERACTIVE SONGS AND/OR ACTIVITIES: Ask the children to approach their grandfriends to find out what foods the Pilgrims and Indians gathered and ate for that historic meal in 1621 (Deer, corn, apples, turkey, potatoes.) Then grandfriends should serenade the children with the song "Bringing in the Sheaves" after you explain the necessary harvesting of fruits and grains.

Thankful Living

Sowing in the morning, sowing seeds of kindness,
Sowing in the noontide and the dewy eve,
Waiting for the harvest and the time of reaping.
We shall come rejoicing, bringing in the sheaves.

Bringing in the sheaves, bringing in the sheaves.
We shall come rejoicing, bringing in the sheaves,
Bringing in the sheaves, bringing in the sheaves.
We shall come rejoicing, bringing in the sheaves.

As the pilgrims and Indians gathered at the first Thanksgiving table they were extremely thankful. Sing the "Thankful Song" now to the tune of "Frere Jacques."

We are thankful, we are thankful,
Yes, we are. Yes, we are.
We are very thankful, we are very thankful.
Yes, we are, yes, we are.

Children should approach their grandfriends and ask, "What are you thankful for?" Then bring the answers back to the microphone. Let the grandfriends interview the children with the same question. Repeat the song with pride.

MARCH/MOVEMENT: Children march to the music of "Turkey in the Straw" with grandfriends rhythmically clapping. Go back the other way since turkeys don't always go the same direction. Once children become familiar with the melody they can sing "gobble, gobble. gobble" to the tune.

COOL DOWN: Everyone seated. Bring out a large poster board and gather the facts contributed today of nouns or verbs for which people were grateful. Use the letters of T-H-A-N-K-F-U-L so that everyone is thinking about words that start with letter T, for example. List several in each category. Post for all to enjoy.

CLOSING MUSIC: Your favorite.

ANNOUNCMENTS: Continue living with "an attitude of gratitude" everyday, not just on the official holiday. Have everyone ask their friends the question "What are you thankful for?"

Thankful Living

ADAPTATIONS FOR TWO-YEAR-OLDS

Preparation: Pictures of holiday foods, music to "Did You Ever See a Lassie"?

Interactive Songs and/or Activities: Eliminate "Bringing in the Sheaves." While singing "The Thankful Song" have the adults only sing the words "We are Thankful" with the children responding in song with "Yes, we are, yes, we are" loudly. Use holiday food pictures for identification and conversation between generations. Encourage anyone to do the actions to the adapted song "Did You Ever See a Lassie."

Did you ever see a turkey, a turkey, a turkey,
Did you ever see a turkey go this way and that.
Trot this way, trot that way, trot this way, trot that way,
Did you ever see a turkey trot this way and that.

Other verses:
2. Did you ever see an Indian dance this way
3. Did you ever see a Pilgrim walk this way. (arms stiff at side, legs walk stiffly)

Cool Down: Shorten the activity to using the letters of T-H-A-N-K-S. Adult help will be needed. It is fun for the kids to sound out the letters and the grandfriends should be praised for helping with their education.

RESOURCES:

Children's Songbook
   "Frere Jacques" p. 234
   "Ten Little Indians" p. 21
Family Songbook of Faith and Joy
   "Bringing in the Sheaves" p. 130
Mitch Miller Community Song Book
   "Turkey in the Straw" p. 68

Wee Sing and Play Musical Games
   "Did You Ever See a Lassie?" p. 28

For additional ideas see
The Joy of Music in Maturity
   "Thanksliving" p. 411-415
   "Thanksgiving" p. 417-423

"PEOPLE WHO NEED PEOPLE ARE THE LUCKIEST PEOPLE IN THE WORLD"
— from *People,* (Bob Merrill and Jule Styne)

INDIAN HEADBAND PATTERNS

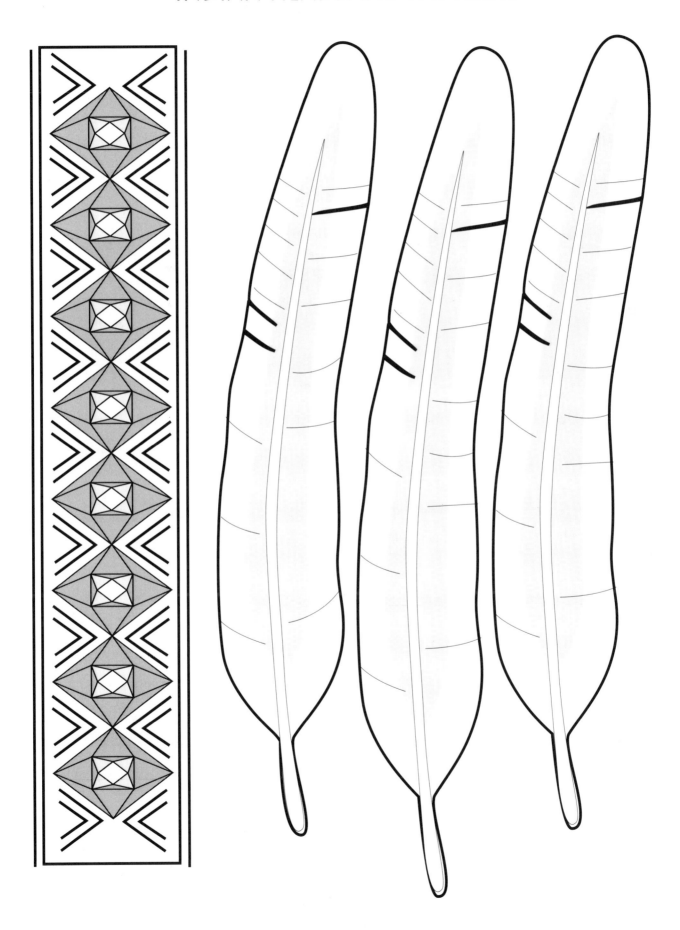

INTERGENERATIONAL SONG SHEET

Bringing In the Sheaves
(ca. 1880)

Words: Knowles Shaw
Music: George A. Minor

Sow-ing in the morn-ing, sow-ing seeds of kind-ness, Sow-ing in the noon-tide

and the dew-y eve, Wait-ing for the har-vest and the time of reap-ing,

We shall come re-joic-ing, bring-ing in the sheaves. Bring-ing in the sheaves, bring-ing in the

sheaves, We shall come re-joic-ing, bring-ing in the sheaves. Bring-ing in the sheaves,

bring-ing in the sheaves, We shall come re-joic-ing bring-ing in the sheaves.

INTERGENERATIONAL SONG SHEET

Turkey in the Straw
(ca. 1834)

Traditional

Oh, as I was a-go-ing on down the road, With a tir-ed team and a great big load, I cracked my whip and the lead-er sprung. So I said good-bye to the wag-on tongue. Tur-key in the straw. (Whistle -) Tur-key in the straw. (Whistle -) Roll 'em up, twist 'em up, High tuck-a-haw, and we'll all sing a tune called "Tur-key in the straw."

WESTWARD HO!

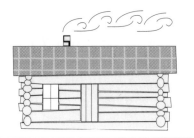

Program 23: WEST

PREPARATION: Items needed include Cowboy hats and/or red bandannas for all, hobby horse for children (pattern included), clip clop blocks and/or rhythm sticks, guitar, pictures of buffalo, antelope, deer (included), and logs to represent a campfire (optional.)

MUSIC: "Home on the Range," "My Pony Boy," "Old MacDonald Had a Farm" with adapted words, "You are My Sunshine," and "Happy Trails" or "On the Trail" from the *Grand Canyon Suite* or "The William Tell Overture."

GREET SENIORS: One on one before the children enter.

RELAXING REHEARSAL: Song review of "Home on the Range" and "My Pony Boy" (music handout.)

> Pony Boy, pony boy, won't you be my pony boy?
> Don't say no, here we go off across the plains.
> Marry me, carry me right away with you
> Giddy up, giddy up, giddy up, whoa! My Pony Boy.

OPENING SONG: Your favorite.

MUSICAL WARM UP: Introduce everyone to the theme of being on a ranch out west complete with cowboys, horses, campfires and music. Ask if anyone has ever been to one and allow discussion time. Pretend there is a campfire with logs arranged appropriately. Children gather around guitarist and all sing the adapted song to the tune of "Old MacDonald Had a Farm."

> Old MacDonald had a ranch, E-I-E-I-O
> And on his ranch he had a _____ (name of animal) horse, cow, sheep, cat, owl.

Complete song traditionally with sounds of animals.

WESTWARD HO!

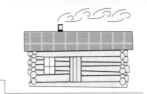

To the tune of "Wheels on the Bus" lead the group in these adapted words (by Verdi Morley) and carry out the actions:

    Verse 1:   Ears on the horse go back and forth…as they prance today
    Verse 2:   Feet on the horse go clip, clop, clip…as they prance today.
    Verse 3:   Tail on the horse goes swish, swish, swish…as they prance today.
    Verse 4:   Nose of the horse goes (blubber with your hand on your lips)
    Verse 5:   Riders on the horse go up and down…as they prance today.

INTERACTIVE SONGS AND/OR ACTIVITIES: Children pass out cowboy hats to grandfriends and then sit down as grandfriends sing a traditional cowboy song "Home on the Range." Use pictures as props of the deer, antelope, buffalo. Discuss these animals as seen in the wild or in the zoo.

The children pass out the rhythm sticks and imitate the rhythm of horses hooves. Leader demonstrates the clip-clop block.

- Everyone should play on the first or accented beat of each measure to the music of "Happy Trails" or "On the Trail."

- In 6/8 time use the same music and play the following rhythm:

When everyone is comfortable with this rhythm announce that the horses are tired and they should follow the slower tempo (if you are playing this on the piano.) Collect all sticks in preparation for the hobby horse march.

MARCH/MOVEMENT: Demonstrate a gallop. Children hold up hobby horse and try galloping in a line around the room. Grandfriends can try the foot movement in their chairs while singing "Pony Boy" or hearing "The William Tell Overture." Arrange for a place for all horses to be rounded up in one location.

COOL DOWN: Return to the campfire scene with children seated and guitarist leading everyone in the song "You are my Sunshine." Explain that this song was originally sung by Gene Autry and Tex Ritter, famous older cowboys often seen in movies and heard on radio.

    You are my sunshine, my only sunshine,
    You make me happy when skies are gray,
    You never know dear how much I love you,
    Please don't take my sunshine away.

WESTWARD HO!

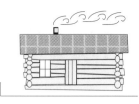

CLOSING MUSIC: Your favorite or "Happy Trails."

ANNOUNCEMENTS: Remind everyone of the beauty of wild life and that it is our duty to protect it.

> ### ADAPTATIONS FOR TWO-YEAR-OLDS
> **Interactive Songs and/or Activities:**
> - Use felt board cutouts to illustrate "Home on the Range" if group is small (patterns included.) Children place items on board as grandfriends sing the song. Pictures may include log cabin, buffalo, deer, antelope, sun, and fences.
> - Use rhythm sticks on accented beat only with strong leadership.
>
> **March/Movement:** Allow children to move freely as they "gallop" their hobby horses to show their grandfriends.
>
> **Optional Activity:** Use a rocking horse for small groups. Children take turns on the horse as it is moved around the circle of grandfriends who help rock the horse. Excellent activity with Alzheimer patients and children.

RESOURCES:

Family Songbook of Faith and Joy
    "Happy Trails" p. 170
Festival of Popular Songs
    "You are My Sunshine" p. 230
Great Music's Greatest Hits
    "William Tell Overture" p. 75
Legit Fake Book
    "Home on the Range" p. 140
    "On the Trail" p. 263
    "Old MacDonald" p. 261
Raffi Children's Favorites
    "Wheels on the Bus" p. 162

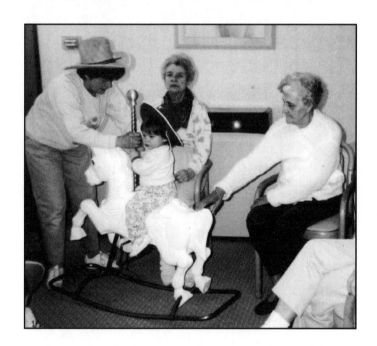

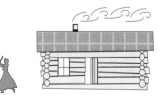

WESTWARD HO!

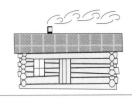

HOBBY HORSE DIRECTIONS:

Materials: Kraft lunch bag, about 4" x 3" x 10", wrapping paper tube, masking tape, broad black marking pen, newspaper.

1. Crumple a page or two of the newspaper and fill the lunch bag.

2. About a third of the way up from the bottom of the bag, wrap a band of masking tape. Pull this entire section in a bit to form the horse's nose.

3. Run a masking tape band perpendicular to the first to the top of the bag, enclosing the wrapping paper tube, and back to the first band. Catch the top of the tube in the bag.

4. Add additional tape to secure the bag to the tube.

5. Add eyes, mouth and nose to the bag using the pen. Ears cut from another bag are optional.

6. Cut four 3" x 12" strips from colorful advertising parts of the newspaper. Staple these together along one edge and fringe them about 2" in from the other side. Fold the stapled strip over and then tape onto horse head to form the mane.

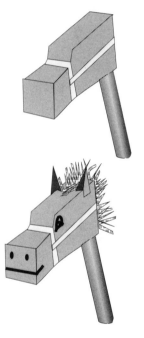

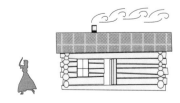

SOME LARGE ANIMALS OF THE WEST

INTERGENERATIONAL SONG SHEET

My Pony Boy
(1909)

Words: Bobby Heath Music: Charley O'Donnell

Po - ny Boy, Po - ny Boy, Won't you be my Po - ny Boy?

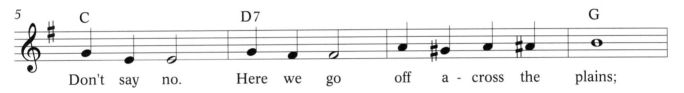
Don't say no. Here we go off a - cross the plains;

Mar - ry me, Car - ry me Right a - way with you.

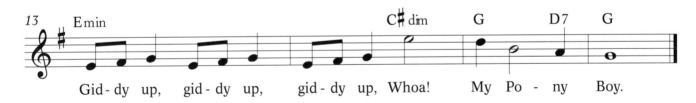
Gid - dy up, gid - dy up, gid - dy up, Whoa! My Po - ny Boy.

Wheels Take Us Places

Program 24: WHEELS

PREPARATION: Items needed include a wheelchair with an oogah horn, safety belt and bag on back to hold a helmet, train whistle, conductors hat, paper plates for everyone to represent wheels.

MUSIC: " Wheels on the Bus" (music handout), "In My Merry Oldsmobile," "I've Been Working on the Railroad," "She'll be Coming Round the Mountain" and "Down by the Station." Recorded music of any transportation songs.

GREET SENIORS: One on one before the children enter.

RELAXING REHEARSAL: Explain theme of "Wheels" that transport us to various places including the use of a wheelchair. Teach the adapted words to "The Wheels on the Bus" song.

> The wheels on the chair go round and round, round and round, round and round,
>   the wheels on the chair go round and round, all through our home.
> The horn on the chair goes beep, beep, beep…
> The belt on the chair keeps us safe…
> The bag on the chair holds our stuff…

OPENING SONG: Use your favorite opening song each session.

MUSICAL WARM UP: Announce the theme to everyone and then ask the children for their ideas on what has wheels that we can ride on. Use their suggestions in the following song (to the tune of "She'll Be Coming Round the Mountain.") Add a tooted horn at the end of each sentence.

> She'll be riding in a car when she comes (toot toot)
> She'll be riding in a car when she comes (toot toot)
> She'll be riding in a car, she'll be riding in a car,
> She'll be riding in a car when she comes (toot toot)

Other verses: replace car with van (which accommodates wheelchairs), train, and tricycle.

Wheels Take Us Places

Exercise: Pass out paper plates to everyone and exercise to the music of "In My Merry Oldsmobile" as follows:

- Driving the steering wheel—exaggerated wheel motions with the plate
- Bumpy road conditions—shoulders and wheel up and down
- Wheels turn in a circle—circle motion with plates

INTERACTIVE SONGS AND/OR ACTIVITIES: Ask the children to collect the paper plates from the grandfriends and stack them up for another trip someday. Sing the adapted words of "The Wheels on the Bus" as taught earlier to the grandfriends. Repeat with the children as a grandfriend points out the object in each verse. Allow the children to sit in the wheelchair, push it or be pushed.

MARCH/MOVEMENT: Children form a train by holding on to the waist of the person in front of them. Leader wears the conductors hat. When ready, have the grandfriends shout "All Aboard!" Someone should blow the whistle. Play the music of "I've Been Working on the Railroad," or "Down By the Station" as the train moves around the room.

COOL DOWN: Everyone can be seated as you inquire about their favorite places to visit that require wheels to get there.

CLOSING MUSIC: Use the same song each session.

ANNOUNCMENTS: Encourage everyone to be grateful for the many forms of transportation available to us including walkers, legs, canes, wheelchairs, cars, skateboards and rockets.

OPTIONAL ACTIVITY: Prepare a large red STOP sign and a green GO sign ahead of time. Children form a large circle and face inward. One child is chosen to sit in the wheelchair. An adult pushes the chair around the inside of the circle. Another adult uses the STOP and GO signs to start the taped music as well as stop it. The wheelchair moves only when the GO sign is up. When the STOP sign is lifted, the wheelchair stops allowing the child next to it to be the next rider.

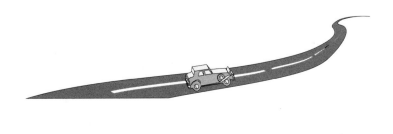

Wheels Take Us Places

ADAPTATIONS FOR TWO-YEAR-OLDS

Substitute the paper plate activity with the adapted words to "The Farmer in the Dell."

I'm going for a ride, I'm going for a ride
I'm on my way to (grandpa's) house (or friend's, to see the zoo)
I'm going for a ride.

Optional—Children may bring small riding vehicles and demonstrate for grandfriends: tricycle, riding car, or fire engines

RESOURCES:

Children's Songbook
"Down by the Station" p. 116
"Farmer in the Dell" p. 232
"I've Been Working on the Railroad" p. 158
"She'll Be Coming Round the Mountain" p. 178

Family Songbook of Faith and Joy
"In My Merry Oldsmobile" p. 194

Raffi Children's Favorites
"Wheels on the Bus" p. 162

Let's do Wheelies!

"IT IS IMPORTANT TO A SENSE OF SELF ESTEEM TO BE ACKNOWLEDGED BY THE YOUNG AS AN ELDER."
— Dr. Robert Butler

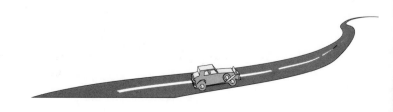

INTERGENERATIONAL SONG SHEET

Wheels on the Bus

Traditional

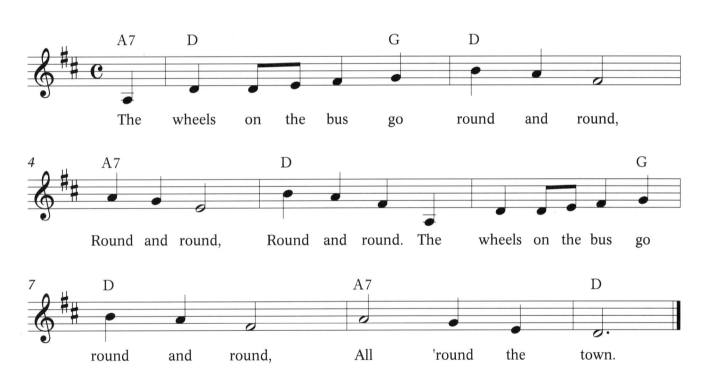

Let It Snow

Program 25: WINTER

PREPARATION: Items needed include paper snowflakes (directions included) glued on a blue paper circle and pasted on a foam paper plate, lots of jingle bells, winter clothing for an adult and child including boots, ski pants, jacket, hat, gloves and muffler, several boxes to hold plates and clothing, three nerf balls, and an outdoor snowman if possible. Be sure to keep a snowball in your freezer for next summer's surprise.

MUSIC: "Over the River and Through the Woods," (music handout) "Frosty the Snowman," "Jingle Bells," and "Here We Go Round the Mulberry Bush."

GREET SENIORS: One on one before the children enter.

RELAXING REHEARSAL: Rehearse just the first part of the song "Over the River and Through the Woods" (music handout.)

> Over the river and through the woods,
> to grandmother's house we go;
> The horse knows the way to carry the sleigh
> through the white and drifted snow.

OPENING SONG: Your favorite.

MUSICAL WARM UP: Talk about activities one can do with snow. Then sing to the tune of "Here We Go Round the Mulberry Bush" this song and follow the actions:

> This is the way we make a snowball, make a snowball, make a snowball.
> This is the way we make a snow ball, on a wintry day.

> Verse 2: This is the way we shovel the snow…on a wintry day.
> Verse 3: This is the way we shiver with cold…on a wintry day.
> Verse 4: This is the way we like to keep warm…on a wintry day.
> Verse 5: This is the way we eat the snow…on a wintry day.

Let It Snow

Group singing of "Let It Snow." Adults sing first three lines. Children finish with "Let It Snow" sung three times.

INTERACTIVE SONGS AND/OR ACTIVITIES: Children pass out snowflake plates. Talk about their uniqueness, how no two are alike. Exercise as follows with music:

"Over the River and Through the Woods"— Move plate like a car window washer to and fro.
"Frosty the Snowman"— Make large circles with the plates.
"Jingle Bells"— Plates go up and down.

Wintertime chant: Teach the chant and then pretend to dress for winter.

> One-two—cover our shoes. (boots)
> Three-four—coats we wore.
> Five-six—caps that fit.
> Seven-eight—mittens are great.
> Nine-ten—it's winter again.
> Let's be tougher with scarves or muffler.

Wintertime clothing: Place one child's and one adult's complete set of outdoor winter clothing in a pile on the floor. Mix it up. Ask for two volunteers who would like to get dressed in winter's warm clothes. Have a child or two dress an adult and an adult dress a child, preferably an adult who never had children—in order to provide a new experience. Ask the group to all make wintry sounds of cold winds—ooooooh during this activity. Take a picture of the proud foursome when completed.

MARCH/MOVEMENT: These four get to lead the wintertime march. Play "Let It Snow" or "Frosty the Snowman" on the piano or tape recorder to accompany the march. Use rhythm instruments with lots of jingle bells.

COOL DOWN: Ask if the wintry child and adult would like to cool down without their wintry clothing and join the seated circle. Ask everyone to close their eyes and picture a warm sunny beach with blue skies. Add to this scenario as you wish. Open eyes and discuss if their imaginations helped them feel warmer.

CLOSING MUSIC: Your favorite.

ANNOUNCEMENTS: Suggest that a person can always warm himself with friendship as well as with winter clothing.

OPTIONAL ACTIVITY: Have the children or adults make an outdoor snowman a few days ahead holding a poster announcing this Winter program or a sign that says "Hi grandfriends."

ADAPTATIONS FOR TWO-YEAR-OLDS

Preparation: Six inch paper doilies, music to "Frere Jacques." Flannel board, winter objects for board, very soft ball.

Musical Warm Up: omit group song "Let It Snow." Use adapted words to "Frere Jacques":

Snow is falling, snow if falling,
All around, all around,
Falling, falling, falling, falling, falling, falling,
To the ground, to the ground.

Children move paper doily snowflakes through the air and drop them on the word "falling."

Interactive Songs and/or Activities: omit the winter clothing activity and replace with a flannel board of various wintry objects such as a shovel, sled, snowball, mittens, or skis.

Consider the use of very soft balls to represent an indoor snowball and toss between generations. If possible bring in a real snowball for anyone to feel.

RESOURCES:

Children's Songbook
 "Frosty the Snowman" p. 240
 "Mulberry Bush" p. 216
 "Frere Jacques" p. 234
Merry Christmas Songbook
 "Jingle Bells" p. 126
 "Let it Snow, Let It Snow, Let It Snow" p. 128
 "Over the River and Through the Woods" p. 136

SNOWFLAKE DIRECTIONS:

1. Fold a square sheet of paper in half (1), in half again at 90° (2) and finally at 45° (3).

2. Cut pieces out of all edges. For best effect cut deeply into the side opposite the point.

3. Unfold for a lovely display of symmetry.

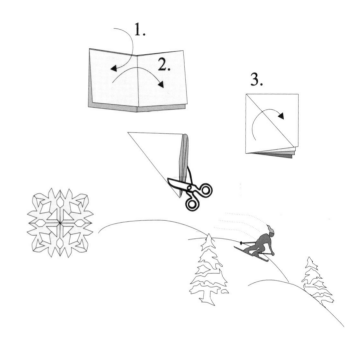

"ALMOST ONE HALF OF THOSE IN INSTITUTIONS ARE CHILDLESS AND MANY HAVE OUTLIVED THEIR AGING CHILDREN."
— E. Brady

INTERGENERATIONAL SONG SHEET

Over The River And Through the Woods

Traditional

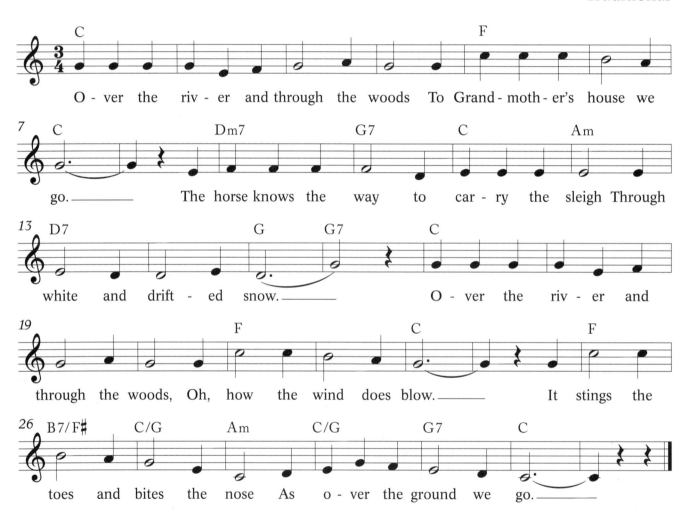

PART THREE
APPENDICES

APPENDIX A
Additional Activities

LARGE GROUP ACTIVITIES
The following activities are suggested to promote additional interaction:

This is Your Life: Feature one resident and celebrate their life by contacting their family for pertinent background information. If you are familiar with this former television show you can pattern your program after it with surprise guests and family members. Use favorite songs of the celebrant, adapt songs to fit the occasion and be sure and include group singing with a handout for everyone to keep. Prepare a special chair of honor that could be decorated by the children. Take photos that can be posted on a tribute board and also given to the honoree in an album.

Balloons: Helium balloons have many uses including their attachment to lightweight things that can float around the room. Also, they are good for releasing all at once from inside an old sheet to celebrate an event. Attach with string to furniture during programs. Batting fun between the children and their grandfriends is best at eye level when balloons are anchored to a bean bag. Coordinate the colors with your thematic program for a beautiful sight. Give them away as a memento. Make sure there are enough for everyone since they are popular.

Air filled balloons are great for tossing. Let the children deliver them to their grandfriends. Enjoy passing back and forth. Talk about colors. Be prepared for children squeezing them and making balloon sounds. Hiding the balloons for the kids is fun for everyone to witness. In lieu of budget restrictions or unavailability of helium, substitute air filled balloons for decorating. Their visual impact is always impressive. Complete silliness is achieved by letting the kids sit on them. POW.

Scarves: Collect silk scarves or alter large scarves to approximately 12" x 12". If one color is preferred for a particular program, buy a large remnant and cut to a reasonable size for use in simple exercises to music. Scarves should be placed in baskets that the children can distribute. Use with different tempos of music such as two step, waltzes, marches and any music that is free and floating. A leader is necessary to be effective in exercising in unison with the tempo. Also, encourage free expression and praise the results. As a finale, let the scarves float upward and then gently to the floor. Collect and store for future activities.

Love Day: Any day can be publicized and celebrated as Love Day in addition to Valentine season. Invite teenagers from a local school or church to be a link in the generations. Ask everyone to wear something red that day even if it is just a ribbon. Plan on an activity together, group singing, performances from each generation, Polaroid pictures to take home, red helium balloons for decoration and souvenirs. Serve refreshments. Let music be a major link in this program by singing "Small World" and "It's Love that Makes the World Go Round." Also effective is "If You're Happy and You Know It" with adapted words. To the tune of "Where is Thumpkin" sing "Where are the teenagers?" and continue asking the whereabouts of other age groups, staff, administrators, and optimists.

Appendix A

Bubbles: Always a popular activity. Give everyone the opportunity to blow bubbles or use one of the modern bubble wands in various shapes and sizes. Use background music such as a pretty waltz or the song "I'm Forever Blowing Bubbles." Children enjoy chasing and popping them. Take time to inspect the colors in the bubbles and talk about them. Arrange for a large fan to spread the bubbles throughout the room. Never use straws unless you want a disaster.

Banners: Banners relative to your activity are great for marching and promoting your program around the facility at the same time. Use any of the visual aids in this book or other pictures that can be colored. Attach them to dowels or rhythm sticks. This makes a good project earlier in the week for either age group or as an intergenerational activity. At the same time, it helps to build enthusiasm for the next program. Mini-banners can be waved while marching between the grandfriends. They can be kept or stored easily.

Floaters: Stock your supply area with tissue paper that can be cut to small sizes for programs. Interesting shapes such as snowflakes, stars or leaves can be cut and used to float easily. They spin and turn as they are dropped to the floor. Coordinate this activity with a song related to the object.

SMALL GROUP ACTIVITES

Musical Instruments: Intergenerational cooperation is your goal as child and adult share an instrument that requires striking with the hand or a beater. Take turns holding and producing the sound. Try a drum and beater, two sticks, or tambourine and a hand. Adult guitar players can let the child strum the instrument while they hold and/or finger it. Omnichords and autoharps are good too.

Movement Circle Game: Use ribbon or elastic bandage that has been sewn into a circle. With everyone seated in a circle, alternate a child and an adult. The leader encourages everyone to hold on to the elastic and follow his or her directions. Use movements such as "up and down," "in and out," and "sideways." Use to recorded music or your own directions with background music. This is ideal for movement, coordination, educational directions and cooperation.

Fish Pond: Cut fish (Appendix D) out of construction paper and put a large paper clip in its mouth. Create a pond in the middle of your group with blue paper or a child's empty wading pool. Pole is made with a small magnet at the end of the line. Child and grandfriend can fish together or people can take turns around the circle. Coordinate with a song such as "The Three Little Fishes," or "Under the Sea." Variations could be different shapes, colors, numbers or letters that could be fished and talked about. Use music.

Cut Outs: Cut animals, objects, or shapes that relate to songs such as a variety of animals in the song "The Farmer in the Dell." They can be cut from paper, colored with crayons or markers and then laminated. Pass these out to the grandfriends. As each object is mentioned in the song, name one child to find it. The cut out can be brought to the leader and attached to a flannel board. (Appendix D) They can also be made from felt which sticks to adult clothing easily. Use for stories or nursery rhymes as well as songs.

APPENDIX B
Hello and Goodbye Songs

The More We Are Together (tune: "O Du lieber Augustin")

    The more we are together, together, together,
    the more we are together the happier we'll be.
    There's_____, and _____ and _____ and _____,
    (fill in personal names)
    the more we are together the happier we'll be.

Good Morning to You (tune: "Happy Birthday")

    Good morning to you, good morning to you,
    Good morning_____ (everybody, dear grandfriends, dear children)
    Good morning to you.

Say Hello Song (tune: "When the Saints Come Marching In")

    Oh, here we are—to say hello
    Oh, here we are to say hello.
    And we hope to get to know you
    here we are to say hello.

    Stretch out your hand—to give me five.
    Stretch out your hand to give me five.
    Oh, it's great to be alive.
    stretch out your hand and give me five.

    Oh now it's time, oh now it's time
    Oh now it's time to say goodbye
    And we're glad we got to know you,
    but it's time to say goodbye.

Wave to Say Hello (tune: "Clap Your Hands Together")

    Wave, wave, wave your hand,
    wave to say hello; (goodbye)
    wave, wave, wave your hand,
    Grandfriends (children) (let's all) say hello.

I Know You (tune: "Farmer in the Dell")

    I know _____(names), you know _____,
    Hi ho good morning Oh we all know _____.

    Goodbye _____, goodbye_____,
    Now it's time to say goodbye to our friend_____.

Appendix B

Where are the Grandfriends? (tune: "Where is Thumbkin?")

> Leader:
> Where are the _____ (grandfriends, children, volunteers, sleepyheads, smilers)
> Where are the _____
>
> Response:
> Here we are, here we are (wave when appropriate)
>
> Leader:
> How are you today friends?
>
> Response:
> Very well we thank you,
>
> Leader:
> God Bless You, (good morning to you)
>
> Response:
> God Bless You.

Make New Friends

> Make new friends but keep the old,
> One is silver and the other gold.

Hello Children (tune: "Goodnight Ladies")

> Hello children, hello children, hello children (Or change to goodbye)
> We're glad you came today.
>
> Hello grandfriends, hello grandfriends,
> Hello grandfriends, hello, hello, hello.
>
> Merrily we sing along, sing along, sing along,
> Merrily we sing along, hello, hello, hello.

MUSIC RESOURCES:

Children's Songbook
 "Farmer in the Dell" p. 232
 "Happy Birthday to You" p. 252

Sing a Song with Charity Bailey
 "Hello Everybody"

Very Favorites of the Very Young
 "The More We are Together" p. 2

Wee Sing Around the Campfire
 "When the Saints go Marching In" p. 24
 "Make New Friends" p. 45

Wee Sing Children's Songs
 "Clap Your Hands" p. 12
 "Good Night" p, 50
 "Where is Thumbkin?" p. 17

# INTERGENERATIONAL SONG SHEET

Welcome Song

Source unknown

Hello, Everybody

Words and music: Charity Bailey

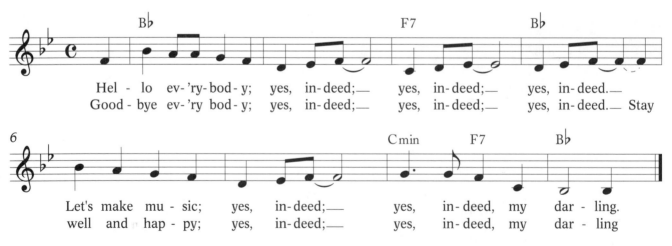

APPENDIX C
Useful Form Letters

SAMPLE LETTER FOR PHOTOGRAPHY PERMISSION

Dear Parent,

Our lively Intergenerational Music Therapy programs need to be captured on film and sometimes on video. May we have permission to photograph your child in action during these sessions? Photos will be posted on bulletin boards, placed in scrapbooks and given to you, if requested. If used for local newscasts or published outside our facility, we will inform you. Please sign the release form below and return it as soon as possible for our files.

_____ has my permission to photograph my child during the
            (Facility name)

Intergenerational Music Therapy sessions. This permission is effective for a period of one year. I understand that I will be contacted personally if photographs are used by the outside media. The preferred name and spelling for my child should read as follows:

_____.

(Print name, including family name if desired)

Signed_____

Date_____

SAMPLE LETTER FOR SPECIAL PARTICIPATION

Dear Parent,

_____ will be participating in an Intergenerational Music Therapy program at
    (Child's name)

_____on _____at _____.
    (name of facility)   (date)   (time)

It is requested that your child bring_____

to share in this program. Leaders of these sessions have found that sharing special possessions related to the program theme helps to promote interaction between the generations. You and your family members are always welcome to participate in these worthwhile programs.

Signed_____

Title_____

APPENDIX D
Multi Use Patterns

DIRECTIONS FOR FELT BOARD

1. Obtain a 2' by 2' or 2' by 4' ceiling tile from a hardware or building supply store.
2. Stretch a piece of felt over the front surface with enough material to extend about an inch on the back of all sides.
3. Attach this all around the back using a staple gun with the longest available staples which don't come out the front—at least 3/8". For extra durability glue can be spread on these back edges before the stapling is done.
4. Any light weight object can be attached to the felt board by gluing areas of felt to their backs. Examples include paper, felt or cloth cutouts, streamers, laminated or plastic objects, photos, foil objects, flags, etc.
5. Save your felt board and the display items for future programs.

FAN

1. Accordion fold a sheet of wallpaper sample or other heavy paper. For adults it should be about 8" by 10" and for children about 5" by 7". A simple way to get even folds is to fold in half, then that in half again at least 2 and preferably 3 times. The result will not have the alternate directions of the folds but the ones which are wrong are easily reversed.
2. Spread the sheet out again and then gather the folds along one edge to form the fan.
3. Tape the gathered end.

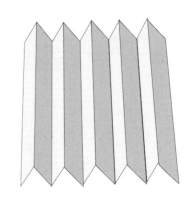

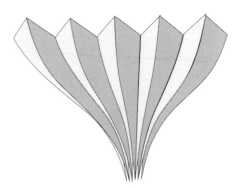

Some Fruits for the Felt Board

Appendix D 149

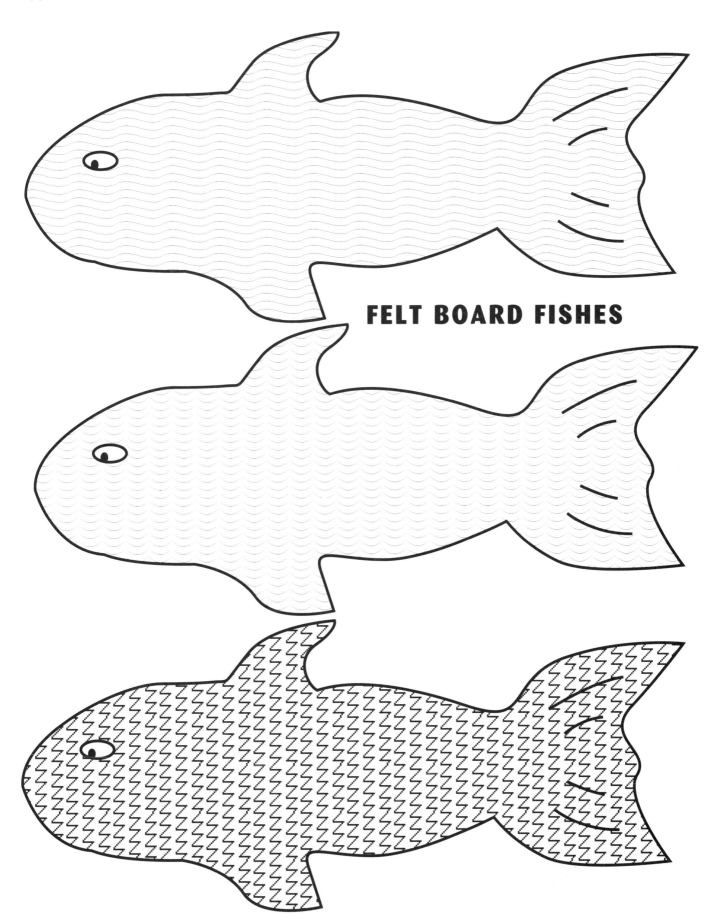

FELT BOARD FISHES

APPENDIX E
Photo Album

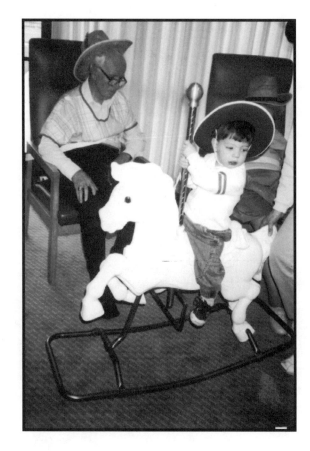

PART FOUR
RESOURCES

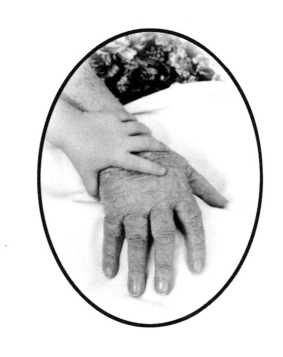

RESOURCE LISTS

MUSIC BOOKS

All American Songbook. Miami, FL, 1984: Big Three Publications (CPP Belwin)
Children's Songbook. Pleasantville, NY, 1988: Readers Digest
Disney Collection. Milwaukee, WI, 1990: Hal Leonard Publications
Family Songbook. Pleasantville, NY, 1981: Reader's Digest
Family Songbook of Faith and Joy. Pleasantville, NY, 1981: Reader's Digest
Festival of Popular Songs. Pleasantville, NY, 1991: Reader's Digest
Great Music's Greatest Hits. Pleasantville, NY, 1982: Reader's Digest
Greatest American Songbook. Milwaukee, WI, 1991: Hal Leonard Publications
Legal Fake Book. Miami, FL, 1979: Warner Brothers Publications
Legit Fake Book, edited by R. Wolfe. Miami, FL, 1990: CPP Belwin
Merry Christmas Songbook. Pleasantville, NY, 1981: Reader's Digest
Mitch Miller Community Songbook, edited by G. Freedman. New York, NY, 1962: Remick Corp.
New Words, Old Tunes. Rita Shotwell, Van Nuys, CA, 1988: Alfred
Piggyback Song Series, Peggy Warren. Everett, WA, 1985-1995: Warren Publishing House
Popular Songs That Live Forever. Pleasantville, NY 1982: Reader's Digest
Raffi Children's Favorites. New York, NY, 1993: Amsco Publications
Real Little Best Fake Book Ever. Milwaukee, WI, 1992: Hal Leonard Publications
Rhythm and Movement Activities–Early Childhood, Rita Shotwell. Van Nuys, CA, 1984: Alfred
Treasury of Best Loved Songs, Pleasantville, NY, 1989: Reader's Digest
Ultimate Fake Book, Milwaukee, WI, 1981: Hal Leonard Publications
Wee Sing and Play Musical Games. Los Angeles, CA, 1986: Price, Stern, Sloan
Wee Sing America. Los Angeles, CA, 1988: Price, Stern, Sloan
Wee Sing Around the Campfire. Los Angeles, CA, 1984: Price, Stern, Sloan
Wee Sing Children's Songs. Los Angeles, CA, 1986: Price, Stern, Sloan
Wee Sing Nursery Rhymes and Lullabies. Los Angeles, CA, 1985: Price, Stern, Sloan
Wee Sing Silly Songs. Los Angeles, CA, 1984: Price, Stern, Sloan
1001 Jumbo Words and Music. Las Vegas, NV, 1985: TVegas Songs Inc.

INTERGENERATIONAL BOOKS

Goals, needs and preparations for intergenerational programs are all in the reference section following Part One, Chapter One, of this book. Brief descriptions of the books and research papers are included. Practical preparation for intergenerational programs are included at the end of Chapter Two of this book. All references deserve further exploration.

The following are useful for expansion of intergenerational involvement in addition to the preschool age group covered by Musical Bridges. There are many excellent programs and resources are available. None, however, involve music specifically.

Becoming a School Partner: A Guidebook for Aging. Washington D.C., 1992: AARP and NAPE.
    Intergenerational partnerships in schools including the twelve stages of program development. Obtain from either the American Association of Retired Persons (AARP), 601 E. Street NW, Washington, DC. 20049 or the National Association of Partners in Education (NAPE), 209 Madison Street, Suite 401, Alexandria, Virginia, 22314

Clay, Rebecca: *Intergenerational Projects Idea Book,* Washington, DC. 1993: AARP

A description of 94 existing programs in place from basic tutoring to corporate day-care centers. This publication lists both intergenerational organizations and available publications.

Erdman, Palmore, ed.: *Handbook on the Aged in the United States.* Westport, CT, 1984: Greenwood Press.

Statistical tables, demographics on various religious, ethnic groups and special concerns including those in health care facilities.

Generations Together: An Intergenerational Studies Program. Pittsburgh, PA 1993: University of Pittsburgh.

This is an intergenerational publications catalog that includes information on programming for scool, exceptional children and the arts. This catalog, along with the periodical *Exchange* , can be obtained from the University Center for Social and Urban Resources, University of Pittsburgh, 121 University Place, Suite 300, Pittsburgh, PA 15260-5967.

Weiner, Marcella, Brok, A., Snadowsky, A.: *Working with the Aged: Practical Approaches in the Institution and Community,* Englewood Cliffs, NJ, 1979: Prentice Hall, Inc.

This book covers normal personality development in old age, sensory training, re-motivation techniques and additional therapeutic approaches.

Wilson, Janet O., compiler: *Connecting the Generations: A Guide to Intergenerational Resources.* Pittsburgh, PA. 1994: University of Pittsburgh.

An overview of intergenerational programming with selected lists of books, manuals and medical resources.

ADDITIONAL RESOURCES

ElderSong. Mt. Airy, MD 1996: ElderSong publications.

Free catalog listing creative activities, materials and music for older adults. Also a music and gerontology bi-monthly newsletter. $15 year. Write Becky Karras RMT, editor and publisher, P.O. Box 74, Mt. Airy, MD

Creative Arts Therapy and General Music Education Catalog. St. Louis, MO, 1995: MMB Music, Inc.

Free catalog that lists popular books for Exceptional Children, Music Therapy, Art Therapy, Dance/Movement Therapy, Physically Challenged, Geriatric resources, and Arts Medicine. Also General music, Kodaly, Orff-Schulwerk, Musical plays, Song collections, Instruments, Records and Cassettes. Write: MMB Music, Inc., Contemporary Arts Building, 3526 Washington Ave., St. Louis, MO 63103

Learning From the Past Madison, WI, 1992: Bi-Folkal Productions Inc.

Guide to using Bi-Folkal kits for intergenerational settings. Covers themes, books, audio visual aids, possible research topics, projects, and instructional objectives. Write Bi Folkal Productions, 809 Williamson Street, Madison, WI. 53703

QUOTATION SOURCES
(Listed in order of appearance in text.)

"A SOCIETY THAT CUTS OFF OLDER PEOPLE FROM MEANINGFUL CONTACT WITH CHILDREN...... IS GREATLY ENDANGERED. IN THE PRESENCE OF GRANDPARENT AND GRANDCHILD, PAST AND FUTURE MERGE IN THE PRESENT." — *Margaret Mead*
   as quoted by M. Crites in *Blackberry Winter* p. 282, New York, NY, 1989: Haworth Press.

"WE MUST BRIDGE THE GAP OF YOUNG AND OLD BY ENCOURAGING ALTERNATE FORMS OF SOCIAL ORGANIZATION TO SUPPLEMENT THE FAMILY STRUCTURE FROM WHICH YOUNG AND OLD ARE OFTEN WITHDRAWN." — *Patrick Ginnane*
   from White House Conference on Aging, 1971.

"HOW OLD WOULD YOU BE IF YOU DIDN'T KNOW HOW OLD YOU WAS?"
— *Satchel Paige, when asked the profound question of his age.*
   as quoted by Hugh Downs in *Thirty Dirty Lies About Old*, p. 13. Niles, IL, 1975: Argos.

"PERHAPS THIS IS THE MOST IMPORTANT FUNCTION OF MUSIC—TO GIVE WHOLENESS TO AN EVENT AND CONVEY A SHARED MOOD." — *Margaret Mead*
   from *Margaret Mead: Some Personal Views,* Edited by Rhoda Metraux, p. 232. New York, NY, 1979: Walker and Co.

"IF THE FUTURE IS TO BE REALLY ACCEPTED, IT MUST BE ANCHORED IN A FEELING FOR THE PAST."— *Margaret Mead*
   from *Surrounded by Angels* as quoted by Yvonne Mersereau and Mary Glover in *Language Arts,* April 1990.

"ADULT DAY CARE ADDS TO CONTINUAL INDEPENDENCE, CAREGIVERS BENEFIT, STIMULATES EVEN ALZHEIMER'S VICTIMS, RELIEVES DEPRESSION AND ALSO ISOLATION."
— *Hugh Downs*
   from *Thirty Dirty Lies about Old,* by Hugh Downs, p. 132. Argos IL 1975

"GENERATION CAN MEAN AGE GROUP, BIRTH COHORT OR LINEAGE WITHIN FAMILIES."
   from *Ties That Bind,* by Kingston, E., Hirshorn, B., and Cornman, J., p. 39. Washington, DC, 1986: Seven Locks Press.

"THE 'ELDER FUNCTION' REFERS TO THE NATURAL PROPENSITY OF THE OLD TO SHARE WITH THE YOUNG THE ACCUMULATED KNOWLEDGE AND EXPERIENCE THEY HAVE COLLECTED."
— *Dr. Robert Butler*
   from *Aging and Mental Health: Positive Psychosocial Approaches,* by Dr. Robert Butler, p. 24. St. Louis, MO: C.V. Mosby Co.

"THE OUTSTANDING CHARACTERISTIC OF THE ELDERLY, NOW AND IN THE FUTURE, IS THEIR DIVERSITY. THERE IS NO SUCH THING AS A 'TYPICAL OLDER PERSON.'"
   from *Ties That Bind,* by Kingston, E., Hirshorn, B., and Cornman, J., p. 39. Washington, DC, 1986: Seven Locks Press.

"THE CONTINUITY OF ALL CULTURE DEPENDS ON THE LIVING PRESENCE OF AT LEAST THREE GENERATIONS." — *Margaret Mead*
   from *Culture and Commitment,* p. 3. New York, NY, 1970: Natural History Museum Press.

"VERY LITTLE DATA EXISTS TO COMMENT ON THE VALUE OF BRINGING CHILDREN AND SENIORS TOGETHER. STILL SOME EXPERTS HAVE NOTICED A SPECIAL BOND BETWEEN CHILDREN AND ELDERS." — *Hugh Downs*
   from *Fifty to Forever* by Hugh Downs, Chapter 7: Home Away from Home, p. 147. Nashville, TN 1994: Thomas Nelson.

"PEOPLE WHO NEED PEOPLE ARE THE LUCKIEST PEOPLE IN THE WORLD"
   from *People*, Bob Merrill words, Jule Styne music 1964

"IT IS IMPORTANT TO A SENSE OF SELF ESTEEM TO BE ACKNOWLEDGED BY THE YOUNG AS AN ELDER."
   from *Aging and Mental Health: Positive Psychosocial Approaches,* by Dr. Robert Butler, p. 24. St. Louis, MO: C.V. Mosby Co.

"ALMOST ONE HALF OF THOSE IN INSTITUTIONS ARE CHILDLESS AND MANY HAVE OUTLIVED THEIR AGING CHILDREN." — *E. Brady*
   from *Aging: Research and Perspectives, Social, Economic, and Environmental Issues Relating to Aging,* by E. Brady, Columbia Journalism Monograph, Nov. 3, 1979

PART FIVE
INDEX

SONG TITLE INDEX

The following list of music was used or adapted for programs in this book. Numbers following the song title indicate the exact program. A song title in bold italics indicates that it is printed music which can be used as a handout.

A-Tisket, A-Tasket	2, 6
All Night, All Day	10
Alphabet Song	17, 18, App. B
Angels We Have Heard On High	12
Ants Go Marching, The	***20***
Apples and Bananas	21
April Showers	20
Army Air Corps Song	12
Autumn Calling	***9***
Baa, Baa Black Sheep	1
Baby Beluga	13
Baby Bumblebee	20
Baby Face	10
Battle Hymn of the Republic	21
Bingo	2, 3, 17, 18
Blue Bird	4
Blue Danube Waltz	4, 7
Birthday Cake Song	5
Brahms' Lullaby	9, 10
Bringing in the Sheaves	***22***
Bye Bye Blackbird	4
Chinatown, My Chinatown	6
Clap Your Hands Together	App. B
Come Josephine in My Flying Machine	12
Count Your Fingers	14
Daring Young Man (on the Flying Trapeze)	7, 12
Did You Ever See a Lassie?	17, 22
Do-Re-Mi	17, 18
Don't Sit Under the Apple Tree	2, 21
Down by the Station	24
Eentsy Weentsy Spider	20
Enjoy Yourself, It's Later Than You Think	3
Falling Leaves	***9***
Farmer in the Dell	1, 7, 24
For He's a Jolly Good Fellow	13, 14
Found a Peanut	20
Frere Jacques	2, 9, 10, 14, 22, 25
Frosty the Snowman	25
Good Morning to You	App. B
Goodnight Ladies	16
Hail to the Chief	***5***
Happy Birthday	4, 6, App. B
Happy Trails	23
Happy Wanderer	16
He's Got the Whole World in His Hands	
	10, ***13***, 14
Hello Children	***App. B***
Hello Everybody	***App. B***
Hello Dolly	8
Here Comes a Funny Ghost	***13***
Here Comes Peter Cottontail	13
Here We Go Round the Mulberry Bush	
	2, 9, 15, 17, 21, 25
Hey Diddle, Diddle	1, 9, 19
Hickory Dickory Dock	1
Hokey-Pokey	20
Home on the Range	23
Hot Cross Buns	3, 5, 12, 21
Hush Little Baby	10
Ida, Sweet as Apple Cider	***2***
I Know You	App. B
I Love You	10, 16
I Love You Truly	16
If You're Happy and You Know It	8, 14, ***15***, 17
I'm Forever Blowing Bubbles	12
In My Merry Oldsmobile	24
In the Shade of the Old Apple Tree	9
In the Good Old Summertime	3
It's Love That Makes the World Go Round	***16***
I've Been Working on the Railroad	24
Jingle Bells	1, 25
Jumbo Elephant	7
Let It Snow, Let It Snow, Let It Snow	25
Let's All Sing Like the Birdies Sing	4, 12
London Bridge	18
Make New Friends	App. B
March of the Toys	8
Mary Had a Little Lamb	1, 4, 5
Me and My Teddy Bear	1
Mickey Mouse March	1, 10
More We Are Together, The	7, 13
Muffin Man, The	21
My Fingers are Starting to Wiggle	14
My Pony Boy,	***23***
O Du lieber Augustin	16
Oh Where, Oh Where, Has My Little Dog Gone?	1, 8
Oh, You Beautiful Doll	***8***
Old Grey Mare, The	3
Old MacDonald Had a Farm	1, 12, 18, 23
On the Trail	23
On Top of Spaghetti	21
Over the River and Through the Woods	***25***
Peanut Butter Sandwich	21
Pop Goes the Weasel	1

Index

Pretty Baby	10
Ring Around the Rocket Ship	19
Ring Around the Rosy	5, 19
Rock-a-Bye Baby	10, 13
Row, Row, Row Your Boat	7
Rudolph the Red-Nosed Reindeer	1, 12
Santa Claus is Coming to Town	13
Say Hello Song	App. B
School Days	17
She'll Be Comin' Round the Mountain	24
Shine On Harvest Moon	9
Six Little Ducks	4
Skip to My Lou (Cut the Pumpkin)	**13**
Smiles	**18**
Sleep, Baby, Sleep	10
Star Dust	19
Stars and Stripes Forever	7, 11, 20
Supercalifragilisticexpialidocious	3
Swim Song	**21**
Take Me Out to the Ball Game	3, 21
Ten Little Indians	17, 22
There Is a Funny Clown	7
This Old Man	16
Three Blind Mice	1
Three Cheers for the Red, White and Blue	**11**
Too-ra-loo-ra-loo-ra, That's an Irish Lullaby	66
Turkey in the Straw	9, **22**
Twinkle, Twinkle Little Star	3, 19
Wave to Say Hello	App.B
We're Off to See the Wizard	13
Welcome Song	**App. B**
Wheels on the Bus	23, **24**
When Johnny Comes Marching Home	20
When the Saints Come Marching In	13
When You Wish Upon a Star	19
Where are the Grandfriends?	App. B
Where is Thumbkin?	App. B
Whistle While You Work	15
Who Can Find the Valentine?	**16**
Who's Afraid of the Big Bad Wolf?	13
William Tell Overture	23
Would You Like to Swing on a Star?	19
Yankee Doodle	11
Yes, We Have No Bananas	21
You are My Sunshine	19, 21, 23
You Must Have Been a Beautiful Baby	10
You're a Grand Old Flag	11, 12, 17
Zoom Song	12

GENERAL INDEX

Aspects of Aging and
    Musical Applications Chart 9
Before the session 16
Behavioral Characteristics and
    Musical Development Charts 6
Benefits for both generations 3
Benefits for the elderly 3
Benefits for the families of both generations 4
Benefits for the staff 4
Benefits for the young 3
Benefits of Intergenerational Programs 3
Equipment necessary 18
First session 15
General Format 25
General goal x
Geriatric participation aspects 8
Hello and Goodbye Songs 142-143
Initial Encounter
    for the elderly 15
    with the preschoolers 16
Introduction vii
Large group activities 140
    Balloons 140
    Banners 141
    Bubbles 141
    Floaters 141
    Love Day 140
    Scarves 140
    This is Your Life 140
Music therapy goals between generations 11
Needs of preschool children 5
Needs of the elderly 8
Photo Album 150
Practical Planning Ideas:
    Before the Session 16
    For the Session 16
    After the Session 17
Preschool participation aspects 5
Programs
  1. ANIMALS—Animal Fun 26
  2. APPLES—Apples Are A-Peeling 30
  3. BASEBALL—Baseball for All 35
  4. BIRDS—It's For the Birds! 39
  5. BIRTHDAYS—Happy Birthday! 43
  6. CHINESE NEW YEAR—
      Happy Chinese New Year! 47
  7. CIRCUS—Step Right Up! 51
  8. DOLLS—Dolls Are Different 55
  9. FALL—Autumn Calling 60
10. FAMILIES—Baby, It's You 66
11. FLAGS—Our Flag Forever 69
12. FLYING—Flying High 74
13. HALLOWEEN—Boo to You 78
14. HANDS—Hands Are Handy 82
15. JOBS—Helpful Jobs 86
16. LOVE—I Love You 90
19. OUTER SPACE—
    Outer Space Is the Place 104
17. SCHOOL—School Bells 96
18. SMILES—Smiles are Super 100
20. SPRING—Spring Fling 108
21. SUMMER—You Are My Sunshine 112
22. THANKSGIVING—Thankful Living 118
23. WEST—Westward Ho 124
24. WHEELS—Wheels Take Us Places 130
25. WINTER—Let It Snow 134
Prolonging the effects 17
Quotation Sources 154
References
    Chapter One 13
    Chapter Two 24
Resources:
    Music Books 152
    Intergenerational Books 152
    Additional Resources 153
Room Arrangements 18
Session Seating Plan 20
Small Group Activities 141
    Cut Outs 141
    Fish Pond 141
    Musical Instruments 141
    Movement Circle Game 141
Successful Music Therapy Ideas 11
Useful Form Letters
    Sample Letter for
      Photography Permission 145
    Sample Letter for
      Special Participation 146
Visual Aids:
    Airplane Pattern 77
    Ant Headband Directions 115
    A-Peeling Badges 33
    Autumn Leaves 63
    Chinese Lantern Instructions 50
    Clown Hat Directions 54
    Dragon Instuctions for Two-Year-Olds 49
    Farmer in the Dell 29
    Felt Board Fishes 149
    Fruits for the Felt Board 148
    Hobby Horse Directions 127
    Home Team Emblems 63
    Indian Headband Patterns 121
    Large Animals of the West 128
    Martian Headband Directions 107
    Newspaper Hat Instructions 71
    Paper Dolls Chain Pattern 59
    Parage Dragon Instructions 50
    Snowflake Directions 137
    Stars 107
    Sunshine Hat Pattern 116
    Valentine Hearts 93